WHAT
HAPPENED
to our
CHURCHES?

A Collection of 52 Blogs
About Regaining Spiritual Energy

DAVID S. LUECKE

TENTHPOWERPUBLISHING

TENTHPOWERPUBLISHING

www.tenthpowerpublishing.com

Scripture quotations, unless otherwise noted, are taken from THE HOLY BIBLE, NEW INTERNATIONAL VERSION®, NIV® Copyright © 1973, 1978, 1984, 2011 by Biblica, Inc. Used by permission. All rights reserved worldwide.

Cover design by Jennasis & Associates.

ISBN 978-1-938840-22-7

Table of Contents

Getting Started   Page
   1. Why Do People Go to Church?   1
   2. Why Young Adults Went Missing
   3. Look to the Spirit for Spiritual Energy

Chapter 1 Six Perspectives on Regaining Spiritual Energy
   4. Moved by the Spirit   7
   5. Recognizing the Spirit
   6. Discipled by the Spirit
   7. Waiting on the Spirit
   8. Culturally Shaped Experiences of the Spirit
   9. Organizing the Spirit's Fellowships

Chapter 2 Motivated by the Spirit   21
   10. The Holy Spirit Influences Human Spirit
   16. Have You Heard Whispers from the Holy Spirit?
   22. Christ's Advocate Prompts Us
   28. They Were "Full of the Holy Spirit"
   34. How Motivations for Church Life Changed
   40. The Spirit Works Toward Self-Actualization
   46. We Knew Who We Are and Why We're Here
   52. Discover the Forgotten Gospel

Chapter 3 Recognizing the Spirit   39
   11. The Spirit Arouses God-Pleasing Feelings
   17. Look on the Other Side of the Coin
   23. Churches Running Almost on Empty
   29. How Paul Recognized the Spirit
   35. Do Supernatural Miracles Really Happen?
   41. How I Discovered I am a Mystic; You May Be, Too
   47. Look for the Present Spirit to Balance Memory

Chapter 4 Discipled by the Spirit   55
   12. Growing into a Free, Cheerful, Glad and Loving Heart
   18. Stuck at Stage 2, Staying at Stage 3
   24. Growing Closer to God Is like Peak Performance by Athletes
   30. Have You Hit the "Wall" Yet?
   36. What's Your Spiritual Journey?
   42. Moving From Growing in Christ, to Close to Christ,
      to Christ-Centered
   48. What Is Your Spiritual Temperament?

Chapter 5 Waiting on the Spirit   71
    13. Jesus Explains What the Spirit Can Do in Your Life
    19. Practice Denying Yourself
    25. Practice Trusting God in a New Venture
    31. Practice Giving Witness to Your Spiritual Experiences
    37. Practice Conversational Prayer
    43. The Path to a Better Prayer Life
    49. Practice Mindfulness of Biblical Promises

Chapter 6. Culturally Shaped Experiences of the Spirit   87
    14. Do Your Kids Know That Human Life Is Sacred?
    20. Ethnic Churches by the Third Generation
    26. Transcendent and Immanent Church Cultures
    32. Learnings from the One Non-Ethnic Church in Tremont
    38. Suburban Ministries Need To Leave Village Culture Behind
    44. Focus on Your Congregation's Culture
    50. Big Changes in American Culture Are Coming

Chapter 7 Organizing the Spirit's Fellowships   103
    15. Your Congregation Is the Top Soil for the Spirit's Work
    21. Do You Want Your Church Leaders To Be Shepherds or Builders?
    27. The Misunderstanding of the Church
    33. Planting Church's the New Way
    39. Emerging Alternatives to Seminaries
    45. Why Do Some Churches Grow and Others Decline?
    51. A Fellowship Builder's Toolbox

Why Do People Go to Church?

Standing on the sidewalk outside a church after its worship, I asked a young, professional-looking woman why she came to church that morning. Her answer was immediate: "I feel the power of God here." She also explained that this church had reached out to her when she was in juvenile detention.

If you were asked that question, how would you answer and how long would you need to think about it? I suspect many traditional Christians from historic church bodies would struggle, only to come up with some version of, "That's what we do on Sunday mornings," or "This is where my friends are."

When my family and I were members of a large Lutheran congregation that finished an impressive new sanctuary 35 years ago, I noticed that the average attendance reported in the weekly bulletin went down. Almost always a new sanctuary attracts more people. I asked the pastor why he thought fewer were attending. All he could come up with was, "I guess our people are losing the habit." Habit is a very weak motivator for participating in anything.

*

Habit could sustain involvement in earlier more stable times when children accepted the ways of their parents. Obviously we are in a time now of fast social change driven by the increasingly rapid innovations in the technology by which we organize our lives. Few of the youngest generation of adults aspire to carry on the habits of their parents because they have so many new options. One result is the almost complete absence of 20- and 30-somethings in the worship and activities of traditional congregations. The long-range implications for their continued decline should be obvious.

I hope to promote discussion about this and other cultural issues among Christians who care about church life and value the heritage of traditional church bodies. By this I mean church bodies that value their centuries-long heritage. They used to be described as mainline: Episcopalian, Lutheran, Presbyterian/Reformed, Methodist. They are all in decline and are best now described as old line.

I have been a practicing pastor now for almost thirty years, observing what works and what doesn't. My books in recent years have focused on how the Spirit works today. In the Nicene Creed we confess he is the Lord and giver of church life. I am convinced that we in traditional churches need to fine-tune our church cultures and the methods through which we express our beliefs, and to do so in the direction of greater willingness to share our spiritual experiences. If you don't have spiritual experiences in church, why bother going?

The outcome I seek is that those who participate in these discussions will learn better to **Name** our encounters with the Holy Spirit, to **Share** those stories with others, to **Seek** more such fulfilling experiences, and thereby to **Reach** more unchurched.

I have studied these general concerns enough to know that I want to organize my contributions in the blogs that follow into these Six Perspectives on the Spirit: Motivated by the Spirit, Recognizing the Spirit, Discipled by the Spirit, Waiting on the Spirit, Experiencing the Spirit Within Cultures, Organizing the Spirit's Fellowships.

The young woman I mentioned who knew why she went to church was an African-American coming out of a Spirit-oriented, predominantly black congregation in the Tremont neighborhood of inner-city Cleveland. Tremont has become a trendy place attracting young adults. It is packed with church buildings from a former era. I intend to do more "why-do-you-go-to-church" research there, expecting the new generation to tell me why they don't. Tremont is also where I grew up.

If you know of other why-do-people-go-to-church research, let me know.

Why Young Adults Went Missing

A seldom-referenced New Testament passage helps explain why so many young adults are not in Christian churches today.

Referring to a reported case of sexual immorality in their fellowship, Paul earlier had written that the Corinthian Christians should not associate with sexually immoral people. Now he clarifed that he did not at all mean the people of this world who are immoral and sinners. "In that case you would have to leave this world. What business is it of mine to judge those outside the church? Exercise judgement on those inside. God will judge those outside" (1 Corinthians 5: 9-13).

In the last several decades a critical balance shifted in the United States. While the majority still consider themselves Christian, less than half are churched. Yet churches still continue to operate as if the United States is a Christian nation where Judeo-Christian ethics still apply to all. We need now to teach ourselves to think like Paul and the early Christians living in the pagan Roman Empire.

The movement toward applying equal rights to homosexuals and married status to same sex couples happened quickly in terms of social movements. Young adults take these rights as self-evident. Yet what they hear from so many church leaders is, to them, extremely prejudicial, old fashioned and anything but loving.

What is the predictable result?
*

Based on a recent survey, Brian Kinnaman reports on 16-29 year-olds who consider themselves outside Christianity. They are about 40% of their age group. Among them 91% see Christianity as anti-homosexual, 87% as judgmental, 85% as hypocritical, 78% as old fashioned, 75% as too involved in politics, 72% as out of touch with reality. So seen, what could Christian churches offer them? Recognize also that this generation grew up being warned to stay away from priests who might be child molesters.

Church loyalties are swiftly disappearing. The basic Christian challenge in America now is to demonstrate the practical value of biblical beliefs and teaching for daily living. But the audience out

3

One challenge is to help preachers and others who follow the heritage of John Calvin realize that they can no longer presume to project the norms of reformed Christian behavior on the whole nation. Whether or not the United States was Christian at the beginning is irrelevant. We aren't anymore. For churched Christians, applying those norms , in the present culture, takes wisdom and sensitivity based on love, not anger.

Paul and the Christ followers in the early centuries knew how to handle themselves as a small minority in a very hostile culture. They had to base their appeal to others on the quality of relationships developed in their fellowships. Theirs was a loving God who interacted with his people through his special Spirit. Our Christian challenge today is to live and witness like early-century Christians in a nation that is no longer predominantly Christian. To do so would be a radical challenge for many congregations.

Perception is reality in our complicated society. Brian Kinnaman in *UnChristian* presents well the challenge of today. We can learn to respond to the unchurched by acting the way Jesus did. This means reacting to criticism with the right perspective—not dismissing it as unwarranted, not being defined by it, and by considering the below-the-surface motivations. In other words, we have to be defined by our service and sacrifice, by lives exuding humility and grace. If a young outsider can't see Jesus in our lives, it is up to us to solve our 'hidden Jesus problem.'"

Kinnaman is a research associate of George Barna, known especially for his surveys reported in *The Frog in the Kettle*. He used the analogy of a frog which doesn't sense rising temperature until it is cooked to death. The dying of frog-like churches is now happening.

The best way forward is to become much more sensitive to church cultures within changing social cultures.

Look to the Spirit for Spiritual Energy

Think about a church's "spiritual energy" as the total of hours and dollars participants give to the shared life and work of that congregation. Now consider these observations:

a. The Spirit-oriented Pentecostal and charismatic movements continue to expand, and many are shying away from oddities and excesses in their past, like speaking in tongues.

b. Evangelicals are moving toward the theology of Spirit-filled and Spirit-led ministries.

c. Forty years ago 30% of the US population self-identified with mainline denominations; now it is about 15%. Their loss of energy is most obvious in empty pews and buildings.

d. A good way for a traditional church to regain spiritual energy is to focus more on how the Holy Spirit energizes Christian fellowships. Classical Calvinist and Lutheran theology left the biblical teachings on the Third Person of the Trinity poorly developed.

My intent it to offer fresh perspectives on what Jesus teaches about his Spirit and how Paul explains the role of the Spirit in Christian church life. Ultimately the spiritual energy of a church is a reflection of how participants experience the Spirit in their lives. We traditional churches can do a better job of waiting on the Spirit.
*

A modern term gives focus to the Spirit's work. It is "motivation"—the understanding of what moves people into action. There is no clear biblical equivalent. Motivation provides the missing link in the classical theology of justification by grace through faith, not by works. The act of trusting God's love and accepting the free gift of Christ's redemption brings us into the fellowship of the Holy Spirit, who is God's empowering presence. Christ's Spirit works on our hearts and brings new priorities that motivate our behaviors. In addition to being saved as a gift of grace, we can also live by the gifts of the Spirit as a second kind of grace.

My intent is to explore and apply biblical perspectives on the Holy Spirit both in Scriptures and through encounters today. Here are six concepts I invite you to probe with me in future blogs:

Motivated by the Spirit Luke uses phrases like "moved by the Spirit" and "filled with the Spirit" to describe unusual motivation among God's people. Those are described by Paul as love, joy and peace and fruit of the Spirit. Rather than virtues to strive for, they are better interpreted as life-enhancing and God-pleasing motivations.

Recognizing the Spirit The Bible tells us how mightily the Spirit moved at that time. Our confessions of faith declare he still moves today. But how do you know when somebody is moved by the Spirit and not just selfish ambition?

Discipled by the Spirit Discipleship is a key concept for current Protestants. But in my experience discipleship opportunities do not draw much attention. That's because it is a "should" action, usually appealing to guilt. The Spirit grows disciples by shaping their motivations to experience more of what God offers and thus become closer to him.

Waiting on the Spirit By God's grace the Spirit changes us. How do we get more of the Spirit's gifts? The answer is to put yourself in the Spirit's workplace—the fellowship of believers gathered around God's word. Some practices are basic. We can do others that stretch our trust and help us learn self-denial.

Culturally Shaped Experiences of the Spirit The social cultures that shape how we communicate and understand ourselves change over time, especially in America now. To be effective, church cultures over the centuries have changed. This involves seeing beyond our current traditions to remain open to the Spirit's movement.

Organizing the Spirit's Fellowships Jesus taught that the Spirit is not predictable. Yet life together in the fellowship of the Spirit does need structure. The challenge is to adapt institutional structures that remain open to the fresh movement of the Spirit. Many churches made poor organizational decisions in the 20th century that lost focus on the Spirit's energy. We need to get back to the basics of Spiritual energy.

1. Motivated by the Holy Spirit

At their first church convention, the earliest disciples made a policy decision. They announced it in a letter to the rest of the church with this phrase: "It seemed good to the Holy Spirit and to us . . . "

Have you ever seen or heard of a church today that announces a decision with that phrase, "It seemed good to the Holy Spirit and to us that . . ."? I haven't. I suspect you haven't either.

Why not?

I think traditional Protestant churches today no longer think of the Third Person of the Trinity as a vital part of our spiritual life. Yes, he was important in Bible times. But we don't expect much from him today.

*

Thoroughly trained in traditional Lutheran church culture, I recall learning lots of Bible stories and digging ever deeper into church teachings. But I also retain the impression that we were basically on our own to apply this knowledge in daily living. Duty was ever before us, and motivation was by guilt. Salvation was for the next life. There we would have direct encounters with God.

Only in recent decades have I fully appreciated Jesus' explanation that he has come so that his sheep may have life abundantly overflowing *now in this life*. Figuring out what that means has been especially difficult for someone with my background. Thank God the Spirit has an easier time producing his fruit with other believers who learned to expect him.

I don't remember church leaders ever expecting dramatic interventions. Fundraising goals were set rationally (2-3 times annual giving), but campaigns relied on the techniques of group dynamics. We prayed for healings, but no one really expected a supernatural miracle, because that (we thought) does not happen anymore.

Traditional, rational mainline churches have grown and served God well over the centuries with barely a passing reference to the Third Person of the Trinity, who nonetheless had been productive in the background.

But most of those traditional mainline church bodies seem to be withering in the 21st century. Where the Gospel is spreading now is among churches that emphasize direct encounters with God.

About fifteen years ago, the church I serve had to decide how much debt to take on for a building project. How much more growth could we expect? We all recognized that borrowing for the full project was not prudent. After many discussions, a compromise emerged to build just the shell of a second wing and finish it later when more dollars were available. The time came for a vote. The tension was high. To everyone's surprise and relief, the vote was unanimous to borrow a half million more dollars to add the shell. I think everyone in that room realized something special had happened. But unfortunately we had no name for it.

The Holy Spirit was truly present in a special way. If a photo had been made of that moment, I would photoshop in the image of a dove over our heads. We could have (and should have) announced to the congregation for their approval that "It seems good to the Holy Spirit and this board that we enter into contracts for 3.5 million dollars of construction with a new loan for $2 million."

Was the Holy Spirit really there hovering over our heads? In future blogs I will share what to look for to be sure. In this case we can be confident because the results were so good. We hit our fundraising goal. We did finish the shell over the next ten years, and the building is packed with activity. Most basic is that it did build up our fellowship without conflict.

Have you ever experienced a controversial church decision when unexpected unity emerged? That was the Spirit's work.

2. Recognizing the Spirit

The first of the four Great Awakenings in American history happened in the 1730s and 40s. Emotions were so high that western New York state was called the burned over district. Arguably America's greatest theologian, Jonathan Edwards was involved but grew skeptical as the Awakening worked its way out.

That movement brought great controversy. One side emphasized religious emotions as the essence; feeling the love of God was most important. The other side taught that the heart of true religion is right thinking; emotions are fickle and often lead astray.

Edwards was decidedly Word oriented. In his writings he argued against a shallow, human-oriented view of spirituality. He taught to look for these reliable signs of the Spirit's indwelling:
*

- A new spiritual sense reflected in love of God that does not come from self-interest
- A new kind of convicted knowing
- A genuine humility
- A hunger for God and a Christlike Spirit; and
- Christian practice

Flipping channels, many believers occasionally come across high intensity healing services and revivals. Most are usually turned off, sensing phoniness, and they quickly move on. Next time dwell a little longer and apply Edward's reliable signs to identify whether the Spirit is really at work. Before judging, beware that those of us from Northern European descent are easily turned off by high emotions. But that is what many others are used to and seek.

First is whether the leaders are pursuing self-interest. Are they making money? Check on the wealth of the featured speaker/healer. Evidence of self-interest should certainly raise doubt about the Spirit's dominance.

Is there a pervasive sense of humility? When the Spirit is at work he changes hearts to bring a new humility. The Spirit cannot do much with a person who is full of him or herself. Those truly full of the Spirit are hesitant to draw attention to themselves. Be careful with those who claim that the Spirit is telling them to do what they are doing. Be cautious with someone whose personal life does not reflect a Christlike Spirit. Do they practice what they preach?

Cleveland has a healer who I think is genuine. Issam Nemeh is an M.D. with a practice on Cleveland's West Side. He does prayer-for-healing services on a Saturday or Sunday at various local churches. These are made known on his website, but are not advertised. He does treat patients at the normal cost for a doctor's visit. That is how he makes his living. Many claim special relief associated with his prayers.

Since "emotions" can be a highly charged word in traditional ministry practices, we do better to talk about "affections." That word is no longer used much in ordinary English. Edwards defined affection as strong inclinations of the soul that are manifested in thinking, feeling and acting. Affection includes a belief held with strong conviction.

Affections can be either good or bad. The difference is the good lead us toward God and the bad away from God. According to Edwards, questionable affections often go along with prideful, show-off quoting of many Scripture passages, or self-serving eloquent talk, or passionate praise for God, or pharisaical devotion to religious activities.

Consider the perspective of Martin Luther. According to scholar Simeon Zahl, "affections" and the heart were central to Martin Luther's theology of justification and sanctification. For him right motivation and willingness of the heart are far more important before God than right action. Luther recognized that affections and the will can actually be transformed by the Spirit of God. "The love of God is a gift of love which is given by the Holy Spirit."

What do you think about the place of emotions in your faith life?

3. Discipled by the Spirit

The church I serve has the purpose statement "To Make and Grow Disciples." We leaders work hard at bringing about that result. We all agree we have a long way to go.

When that statement was finalized, I quibbled with the wording. Making and growing disciples is the work of the Holy Spirit, who calls, enlightens, sanctifies and gathers all believers together in the Christian church. There is no disagreement with this classical statement of the role of the Third Person of the Trinity.

But organizational purpose statements are supposed to be pithy and short. Do we really have to add the complication of the Spirit's role in discipleship and church life? Yes, I think, for several reasons.
*

In the churches I know "discipleship" is one of those religious words everybody is for, but in practice does not motivate much new behavior. It is guilt-inducing. Who can be against better discipleship? But in churches that emphasize God's grace through redemption in Christ, where is the personal benefit from being a better disciple and why be interested?

Contrast that approach with offering opportunities to grow in personal love, joy, peace, patience and the other products or fruit of the Spirit's work. Such experiences were basic to the Apostle Paul's appeals to followers of Christ in his churches. When he talked about their growth, he highlighted increases in love, joy or trust that were evident. Who would not want to be taught how to receive more of such fruit from their discipleship?

Why is it we almost always hear about only one commission given to Christ's followers—the familiar charge in Matthew 28 to go, make disciples, baptize and teach. Those are doable acts. But in my experience appeals to the Great Commission seldom motivate fresh action.

Why don't we pay much attention to Luke's version in the Book of Acts of what Jesus said at his ascension: "You will receive power when the Holy Spirit comes to you, and you will be my witnesses" here and abroad. Luke was discipled by Paul. Paul learned to recognize the Spirit as God's presence energizing his followers.

In his Gospel Luke records Jesus telling his disciples, "I am going to send you what my Father has promised; wait in the city until you have been clothed with power from on high." Finished with their discipleship training, they went on to disciple others, who grew in the fruit of the Spirit personally. That chain of God's empowering presence went on for two millennia of generations. When it was broken by unfaithful leaders, God's Spirit raised up new ones who met God in his Word and grew in the Spirit.

Waiting on the Spirit can start with recognizing the power of the Spirit when he is at work. Look for hearts that are changing in the context of Father's love and the grace of his Son's redemptive work. His specialty is working on the inner being, the spirit, the heart of those encountering God's truth.

I once preached at one of the rare congregations that in recent years built a new sanctuary. Their church leaders had never made the association between the generous offerings in their capital campaign and the Spirit at work motivating such generosity. Recognizing the Spirit in their midst, that congregation continues to be a bright spot in the dreary decline of our church body.

Jesus promised that the Father will send his Holy Spirit to all those who ask him (Luke 11: 13). That promise is not for whatever you have in mind according to your natural motivations, although the Spirit can start there. The promise is for new motivations focused on love, joy, trust and the other feeling-related products of the Spirit's work in the hearts of Christ followers.

I have yet to meet someone who does not want more of the fruit of the Spirit's work. Getting there is a good reason to take discipleship seriously.

What is your view of discipleship?

4. Waiting on the Spirit

When Jesus ascended he told his disciples to "wait for the power from on high." The Spirit came in a dramatic way 50 days later at Pentecost.

Does the Spirit come today? Many traditional and evangelical churches don't act like it, beyond perhaps an annual Pentecost birthday party. That was then. How does he come now? Other blogs discuss how to recognize the Spirit's subtle movements. How can we wait upon his blessings today?

Think like Zacchaeus. He's the short guy who climbed a sycamore tree so he could see Jesus coming. Jesus then saw him and shared dinner fellowship with him. Jesus comes to us now through the Spirit he and his Father send. Like climbing a tree, we can deliberately put ourselves in the Spirit's workplace.

What will you wait for the Spirit to do in your life? His specialty is changing hearts, transforming the innermost being of those who follow Christ. What he produces there is greater love, joy, peace, patience and other fruit described by Paul, including kindness, trust. Think of these as motivations out of which flow God-pleasing behaviors.

Six practices will put you in the Spirit's workplace: They can be remembered in the acronym GROWTH. **G**o to God in worship and prayer. **R**eceive his word for you, **O**pt for self-denial, give **W**itness to your experiences. **T**rust God in a new venture. **H**umble yourself before God.

*

Three of the six are Basic Practices. The other three are Stretch Practices.

The Basic Practices are: Go to God in worship and prayer, Receive his word for you, and Humble yourself before God. The Spirit always works through people of God gathered around his Word. Regularly join them in congregational worship. Jesus promises that as earthly fathers know how to give good things to their children "how much more will the heavenly Father give the Holy Spirit to those who ask!" (Luke 11: 13).

In your prayers, ask for whichever fruit of the Spirit you desire more of. Humbling yourself before God is basic. He usually can't do much with you when you are full of yourself.

The Stretch Practices are: Opt for self denial, give Witness to your experiences, and Trust God in a new venture. The O could stand for Obey. But motivation by duty does not work well in a grace-oriented church.

When Jesus told the rich young man to sell all he owned, he was giving a stretch challenge, not a command. Jesus challenged his disciples to deny themselves and take up their cross. He gave this riddle: "Whoever wants to save his life will lose it, but whoever loses his life for me will save it." Paul told the Ephesians to submit to one another. Self-denial and submission could become a life-style. But start with one deliberate act of self-denial or submission at least once a week.

Trusting God in a new venture will test your trust in God's provi-dence. A new venture could be as simple as offering to care for a neighbor's children for an afternoon. Or it could be as challenging as helping to plant a new church. I came to Cleveland to plant a new congregation. Early on when it looked like a failure, I spent some intense time in prayer about where to go next. This was a breakthrough in my prayer life. That church plant has just dedi-cated their large new sanctuary in a choice location.

Giving Witness to your personal experiences of the Holy Spirit would be a big stretch for most traditional Christians. Stories of what God has done in your life are much more persuasive than cit-ing Bible passages to people who no longer believe the authority of Scriptures. Almost everyone will be willing to hear personal stories told in the right setting.

What is your reaction to these GROWTH practices?

5. The Spirit in Changing Cultures

In the fourth century the Christian church took a turn that still handicaps traditional churches today. The Roman emperor made Christianity the official religion of the Empire. Most consider this a good development. Institutional Christianity then took on explosive growth.

For ministering in the 21st century that was an unfortunate turn. We old-line churches that honor our European roots carry a legacy that weakens our effectiveness in our present American culture. We didn't need the Holy Spirit to carry on ministry in well established patterns supported by the state. We didn't need spiritually gifted leaders. We lost the determination to seek the special power of the Spirit.

To be a Christian in the first three centuries was an act of conviction.   Once the Emperor gave preference to Christianity, then joining the state church was the smart move for citizens with ambition. Much of that explosive growth was made up of people who were Christians for convenience rather than by conviction. Pastors and bishops were exempted from tax obligations. The temptation to seek this status without conviction must have been great.

Church cultures shaped in the context of institutional Christianity in a friendly environment are now declining. Our challenge is to go back to the earlier mission-oriented church and leadership cultures that worked in a hostile pagan culture.
*
Traditional church cultures emphasized loyalty and faithfulness to the established patterns of life from birth to death. For this rational process the Holy Spirit could stay predictably and comfortably in the background and was even unwelcome if he brought too much change.

The Christian churches that are doing well now emphasize life-defining personal convictions, growth in ministry to others and higher levels of spiritual experiences. The Spirit is essential to this heart-changing work. We need to re-read Paul to appreciate how central the Spirit was to his understanding of church and ministry.

Imagine what that state-church arrangement did for the attitudes of priests and pastors. If you can compel, why bother to attract? I once read of a Lutheran pastor in a German village who decided that fathers really should show up for the baptism of their child. So he would send out a policeman to bring the father to church for that occasion. With attendance expected, why bother to figure out how to make the biblical word relevant to the hearers? Personal spiritual growth of villagers was often unwelcome because it could lead to conflict.

Present church leadership culture is in the process of rapid change. The old way separated leaders as clergy distinct from everybody else, the laity. Paid clergy performed religious duties in traditional settings, like a chaplain. They were not expected to be strong leaders of more effective ministry.

Growing community mega churches exemplify the new. Those leaders are much more aggressive in organizing church life where all are ministers. Many have business experience and emphasize "what works" to foster healthy church life. They look for giftedness by the Spirit to identify leaders, and then bring training to them. A sign of the times is that traditional seminaries are in crisis through lack of enrollment.

I have been using "traditional" to define church cultures shaped by their European origins. Another large category would be "evangelical" churches whose culture is shaped by the American experience of frontier and revivals. They emphasize personal conviction as distinct from passive participation of the established churches. The heart-work of the Spirit is necessary for that. Church observer Ed Stetzer notes that evangelicals are also now moving towards the theology of Spirit-filled and Spirit-led ministries.

In your church experience how much attention was paid to the special work of the Holy Spirit? Future blogs will explore how to develop Spirit-led ministries and leadership within the context of traditional church cultures.

6. Organizing the Spirit's Fellowships

Sometimes they put it in big letters as part of the name of their community church. They are "non-denominational." Why is that phrase so important in naming who that Christian congregation is and wants to be?

The new community church movement that has taken off in the recent decades represents almost all the currently growing Protestant congregations. Most are large. Most are in the suburbs or ex-urbs. Some are growing very fast.

Obviously their participants are not impressed with the existing options for congregations organized by denominational heritage. What is the meaning of this movement, especially for churches with a mainline heritage? It is not as if the community churches don't have a theological commitment. Almost all have conservative evangelical or Pentecostal heritage. After four attempts, a church plant near where I live left "Baptist" out of their name and finally gained momentum to become a large community church.

A basic explanation is that young adults and newcomers see existing congregations as "for somebody else." Indeed, who would think to check out the local Greek Orthodox or Ukrainian Baptist congregation without some previous ethnic loyalty? Why check out the Presbyterian or Lutheran brands if their local congregations have low visibility in the community?

There are at least three organizational choices that help explain how the Spirit is getting God's work done in this new movement.
*

1. One of the principles advocated in the Church Growth movement of the 1980s is that people like to go to church with others like themselves. That's true on the mission field today and it was true in early 20th century America. Then most congregations organized themselves by national origin and language, or by church issues in previous generations. By the third or so generation later those concerns and loyalties are mostly gone.

The new commonality is living in a suburban culture that has emerged among strangers who live a fast-paced life focused on family and are looking for help finding meaning in life. The historic churches typically have a hard time, in everyday language, getting to the fundamentals of living better here and now in this world, not just preparing for the next. Unlike the "moderns" of several generations ago the young today are more open to the supernatural and to the authority of Scriptures.

2. After World War II many congregations chose an organizational structure that seemed to work well without consciousness of the Spirit and the energy he brings. They took on the working structure of social clubs with committees and volunteers as a way to get members "involved." That could work during the great out-migration from the central city to suburbs in the 1950s-70s. It was a poor choice. In the 21st century almost all social clubs are in steep decline.

Healthy congregations today are organizing around ministries where the special energy of the Spirit is more visible and necessary. A new reading of Paul's long-neglected chapter on spiritually gifted ministry (1 Corinthians 12) is rippling through congregational structures. For such ministry the Spirit is welcome and even necessary.

3. Legal incorporation of a congregation is a 20th century movement that makes great sense for governance and stewardship of resources. But the real congregation is the underlying fellowship of the Holy Spirit, whose present energy may have departed decades ago.

Incorporating documents traditionally look backwoods to the origins of their denomination to define how the Spirit worked at a former time. The newer Protestant community-church movement focuses on how the Spirit is working now. They seek informal networks of congregations for growth-oriented ideas and identity. The traditional tightly-defined denominational structure is dead. Congregations look for ideas from churches where and how the Spirit is moving now. These become informal networks.

My interest is traditional congregations in denominations. As I know from experience in my own Lutheran church body, leadership is divided between guardians of old traditions and missionaries looking for new ideas and networks. Which will prevail in the long-run is predictable.

In your opinion, will there be any new tightly defined denominations in the future?

Chapter 2

Motivated by the Spirit

Luke uses phrases like "moved by the Spirit" and "filled with the Spirit" to describe unusual motivation among God's people. Those are described by Paul as love, joy, peace and other fruit of the Spirit. Rather than virtues to strive for, they are better interpreted as life-enhancing and God-pleasing motivations.

Blogs

10. The Holy spirit Influences Human Spirit

16. Have You Heard Whispers from the Holy Spirit?

22. Christ's Advocate Prompts Us

28. They Were Full of the Holy Spirit

34. How Motivations for Church Life Changed

40. The Spirit Works Toward Self-Actualization

46. We Knew Who We Are and Why We're Here

52. Discover the Forgotten Gospel

The Holy Spirit Influences Your Human Spirit

Nicodemus was a prominent Jewish leader who came to Jesus under cover of darkness. He wanted to find out more about this new rabbi who had come to town. Jesus was proclaiming that the kingdom of God was at hand, but no one can see it until he or she is born from on high.

Tell me more, Nicodemus said. Jesus explained, "No one can enter the kingdom of God unless he is born of water and the Spirit. Flesh gives birth to flesh, but Spirit gives birth to spirit."

That phrase, "Spirit gives birth to spirit," can have revolutionary meaning today for traditional Christians from mainline churches.

An appropriate translation of the key verb is "the Holy Spirit *influences* human spirit." Human spirit is one of the words the Bible uses for "soul" or "heart" or "inner convictions." A modern equivalent is "motivation." The Spirit can and will change the motivations of those who are open to him.

*

The annual New Year's resolutions many make show that most people want to change something about how they live. They know the behaviors they want, but their key problem is motivation. A biblical understanding of the Holy Spirit would hold out the hope that the Spirit can really change their personal motivation for better follow-through. The Spirit works his changes best in the context of believers who share God's word and are in a fellowship of the Holy Spirit.

What's revolutionary is to recognize that the supernatural can intervene in the natural. John Calvin taught that we can no longer expect miracles to happen. They were needed in Bible times but don't happen anymore. Few educated Protestants in our modern era are willing to recognize the miraculous. I like the definition of a miracle as an extraordinary event for which there is no natural explanation. After years of searching, I have come to believe that indeed miracles do happen in our times. More on that in Blog 35.

Once you change your worldview to recognize that the super-natural God can intervene in natural life, you can appreciate the significance of Jesus' claim that the Holy Spirit actually changes the motivations of real live people today. Paul tells us that the product of the Spirit's work is the fruit described in Galatians 5: love, joy, peace, patience, kindness, goodness, faithfulness, gentleness and self-control.

Who would not want more of such fruit? Who would not want to live with more love, joy, or peace? In discussions I've led, the first choice for most is patience.

What are those characteristics? Usually they have been seen as virtues. They are then preached as behaviors we are each to pursue in our Christian living. I think they are better described as feelings or affections. Out of changed affections and motivations come virtuous behaviors. The motivations are more important than how these express themselves in specific behaviors in daily living.

The core of the biblilcal Gospel is that we can claim life everlasting through the salvation won by Christ's death and resurrection. Consider how belief in the Spirit's intervention into our human spirit really amounts to additional Good News for living in this world. We are not on our own to become the person God wants us to be. His Spirit helps us.

The kingdom of God Jesus preached will be fulfilled in the next life because of what Jesus did. It is initiated in this life because of what the Spirit does. What a wonderful double Gospel. Actually, recovering the Spirit's present work amounts to recovering the original, but now forgotten, gospel.

What are your thoughts about a "forgotten Gospel" for living life today?

Have You Heard Whispers from the Spirit?

In my workshop on How to Spot the Spirit's Work in Your Life, I present four kinds of encounters with the Spirit. The second is hearing whispers from the Spirit. Usually every small discussion group has someone who can tell his or her story of such an experience.

The other three are special moments in routine life in Christ, perhaps on Easter morning. Another is confronting a major loss in your life, like losing a spouse. Yet another would be a rare but profound awakening, like conversion.

Have you ever had the thought pop in your head that you should go visit a specific person right now? When you get there it turns out you are the right person at the right time to give special help needed right then. One lady told of having such a thought and going to the special person, who happened to need eggs for her baking project and the visiting lady just happened to have them. That visit turned into a special discussion with the baker who also happened to need some spiritual counsel.

*

A man talked about the sudden thought to visit an old friend he had not had contact with for years. He got there within minutes of his friend passing and found a room full of people who had known the end was near. The pastor also was there and led them in reflections on the meaning of death for Christians.

Were those just coincidences? Maybe. But most believers are eager to affirm those thoughts as a whisper of the Spirit. After one of my first workshops the pastor said that one of the best parts for his people was the relief that there was a reason for the "coincidence" they had experienced and were reluctant to talk about. Next time you, the reader, have such an experience, be sure to share it.

Bill Hybels is one of the best preachers and church leaders of our times. One of his books is *The Power of a Whisper: Hearing God. Having the Guts to Respond*.

He tells his personal story of a prompting for parenthood. He was having difficulty communicating with a son. "And suddenly the Holy Spirit whispered, 'Bill if you do not adopt a different approach with this little guy, you might lose him forever.'" He read several parenting books. In one, something rang true in this author's counsel. "With God's whisper still punctuating my thoughts, I thought I would give it a try."

Hybels tells that "the first world-rocking whisper I received from God dealt with helping to alleviate extreme poverty. Admittedly, logic would say that I'd be the last person to care about social-action issues. I am a white Dutch guy of reasonable means who spends his downtime racing sailboats. What do I know of poverty and suffering? Then Hybels goes on to discuss ministry plans that evolved to address that issue.

Bill Hybels writes about How to Know When You Are Hearing from God. "Believe me, I am more than capable of hearing what I wish God were saying rather than what he is actually telling—and perhaps you are too. Discerning God's direction is somewhat subjective, but it's not arbitrary. Even though God's whispers are rarely tangible, there are concrete steps we can take to help us discern if we're hearing from God or hearing from the bad sushi we ate last night."

His advice is to run the prompting through five filters. Is it truly from God? Is it Scriptural? Is it wise? Is it in tune with your own character? What do the people you most trust think about it?

This whole issue of hearing a personal whisper from God is new to me in my traditional Lutheran experience. True, pastors are supposed to receive a personal call into a specific ministry. But it is often treated with a "wink" as practical matters are weighed in accepting the call. I am very thankful that on Monday January 15 1990 at about 3:00 pm I became convinced that I was being called to plant a church in the southern suburbs of Cleveland.

Next time you, the reader, hear a whisper from God, pay attention.

Christ's Advocate Prompts Us

On the evening we call Maundy Thursday Jesus gathered his eleven disciples around a table, perhaps like your dining room table with all the extension leaves inserted. Judas had left. Jesus had a long meandering discussion with those who remained about what was going to happen.

Our church has celebrated the Christian Passover several times on Holy Week. Last time it was led by an Israeli member of Jews for Jesus. The Jewish Passover *seder* format calls for drinking four cups of wine. The third is the cup of redemption, which is when we assume Jesus consecrated the wine and bread to be his blood and body. I noticed last time that after those four cups I was feeling rather mellow. Imagine that as the mood of those twelve gathered around the table.

*

Jesus told them, "I will ask the Father, and he will give you another Counselor to be with you forever—the Spirit of truth. The world cannot accept him, because it neither sees him nor knows him. But you know him, for he lives with you and will be in you. I will not leave you as orphans." (John 14:16)

The key term in Greek is *paraklete*, rendered as "Counselor" above but properly translated as "advocate," like a lawyer who stands beside you and presents your case. In his first letter, John uses that word to describe Jesus as our advocate before the Father. So in that one word *paraklete* we have the job description for Jesus and for the Spirit.

A few verses later in John 14, Jesus teaches that "The Advocate , the Holy Spirit, whom the Father will send in my name, will teach you all things and will remind you of everything I have said to you." The most used symbol for the Spirit is the dove that came down from heaven and sat on Jesus' shoulder at his baptism. I envision the Spirit as sitting on my shoulder whispering godly thoughts into my ear. If you are going to accept the spirit dimension in your worldview, you need also to envision the Enemy sitting on the other shoulder.

I go about my day hearing whispers of the Spirit in one ear and the Enemy whispering into the other. This makes for interesting discussions in my head as the day unfolds. I try to "keep in step" with the Spirit, as Paul encourages in his Galatians discourse on the fruit of the Spirit.

Probably the most helpful part of Jesus' discussion with his followers is his promise, "I will not leave you as orphans." That is a revolutionary truth for classic Protestant theology that basically ignores the Third Person of the Trinity. Calvinists emphasize the First Person, the Father. Lutherans emphasize the Second Person, the Son. The Third Person just does not fit into their understanding of the triune God active today.

Classic preaching expands on our duty as Christians and gives strong encouragement to become more Christ-like. But it usually leave us on our own to get from where we are to where God would like us to be. It leaves us as orphans.

Jesus' promise to send his Spirit to change us is what I call the additional good news, the forgotten Gospel. It is truly revolutionary for traditional Protestants . Paul tells us about the fruit the Spirit works, that is, the product of the Spirit's work in our individual lives. The Spirit grows within us more love, joy, peace, patience, kindness, goodness, faithfulness, gentleness and self-control. Is there anybody who does not want more of those qualities?

The main Good News is that by grace we have eternal salvation when we accept the Second Person who advocates our case before the First Person. The additional Good News is that we are not on our own to become more Christlike. The First and Second Persons send the Third Person, the Spirit, to change our human spirit, our motivations. This almost-forgotten Gospel is that freely by grace the Spirit comes to help us grow closer to God and to experience more love, joy, and peace and the other qualities that make our lives more abundant.

We are saved by grace to live by grace—joyfully.

Does this reading of the functions of the God-in-Three-Persons seem fresh to you?

They Were "Full of the Holy Spirit" and An Emotion

Luke uses a unique phrase in his Gospel and Book of Acts. Eleven different times he describes a follower of God as "full of the Holy Spirit" combined with something else, best understood as an emotion. One of the ways to recognize the Holy Spirit at work today is when a follower of Christ proclaims or acts boldly or with special wisdom.

Luke first used the phrase for Elizabeth, who when hearing that Mary was to be mother of the Messiah, was full of the Holy Spirit and burst out in praise to God. Her husband Zechariah, proud at the birth of his son John, was full of the Holy Spirit and proclaimed praise for the coming Messiah. After the resurrection Peter was the full of the Holy Spirit and boldly proclaimed the Good News to the Sanhedrin. Noting his courage, they marveled that such an illiterate could speak so well. The seven chosen to be food administrators were full of the Holy Spirit and special wisdom.

Have you had a special time when, overcome with emotion, you broke out in praise to God? Or have you had a time when you needed to speak about your faith to someone somewhere, and the right words just seemed to flow out of your mouth? Or can you remember when you came up with a unique idea that solved a problem at church that was recognized as especially wise? Now you have a word for it. Then and there you were full of the Holy Spirit. Gain confidence that the Spirit is leading you. Look forward to his next special visitation.

*

To be full of the Spirit at special times does not mean the Spirit is gone at other times. Like the dove who alighted on Jesus' shoulder at his baptism, the Spirit is sitting on the shoulder of believers, constantly whispering into your thoughts how to keep in step with him as you go through your day, whether you recognize him or not. An old word for the Spirit's nudging is following your conscience.

Paul uses the image of the Spirit being poured out on someone. Think of yourself as a jar receiving the Spirit. But your jar and mine has a hole in it called sin, and our resistance to the Spirit can be strong at times, leaving the jar mostly empty. And then when he is most needed, he comes in a special way, and we become full of the Spirit again.

The Spirit specializes in changing hearts. He works on emotions, producing more love, joy, peace and boldness. Some of his people react with hot emotions. Followers whose heritage is Northern European prefer cool emotions.

Traditional Protestants respond better to the Spirit who comes head first in rational ways. They are cautious about those to whom he comes heart first. The dilemma for traditional rational church leaders is that most people today perceive with the heart first over heady explanations. They listen better when they perceive the leader as someone who cares for them and wants to help them on their way to a better life.

Preferences for recognizing the Spirit seem related to socio-economic-educational level. I have written about my visits to churches in the Tremont neighborhood of Cleveland. The four Hispanic churches seemed full of passion. In one they seemed to be interacting with raw emotions. A congregation from a different heritage seemed very rational but with little passion. They probably had the highest educational level of any of the churches in Tremont. But churches of their heritage seem to be declining the fastest among traditional Protestants.

Churches and their leaders who operate mostly at the head level will probably not fare well in the swiftly changing 21st century. The Christian future belongs to those who with heartfelt convictions can communicate well to those who expect emotions in their church life.

Can you think of a time when you were "full of the Holy Spirit."?

How Motivations for Church Life Have Changed

Most of the New Testament after the Gospels is written about the church life of the first several generations of Christians. What prompted them to come together? Roman cities offered many hundreds of clubs and mystery cults to join, not unlike American cities today. Easiest to understand are the Jews already used to synagogue life who accepted Jesus as the Messiah and moved on to a Christian house church. They acted on conviction.

But Luke tells us there were many non-Jewish God-fearers, too. What motivated them? They probably had the same kind of mixed motives found among church-goers today. Most gathered out of conviction. Others were probably neighbors who liked the fellowship. A few knew they could get a meal. Others sought the protection of the influential leader and enjoyed the status that went with this patronage.

We do know that in the earliest years they regularly shared a meal, during which they usually also remembered the Lord's last supper. We know they were expected to help each other out, because Paul scolded the Corinthians for not taking care of the hungry in their midst.

I am offering these descriptions to illustrate motives within the categories of classic motivational psychology.

*

People are motivated into action by opportunities to satisfy needs they see as basic to a better life. Christian churches in America used to be seen as such a way to a better life. Increasingly they are now being ignored. What changed? Look for a shift in needs that motivate behaviors, especially for newer generations.

The basic categories of needs are as follows: first, needs to satisfy bodily requirements (like food and shelter), and then (in order) for security, affiliation, status and self-actualization. Needs already satisfied do not motivate much new behavior. Over the centuries, Christian churches at one time or another proved effective in satisfying all those kinds of needs.

Meeting bodily needs, the first generations pooled their resources to feed widows in their community. In more recent times, medical missions have been a basic form of outreach in poorly developed countries.

Church life that satisfies the need for security is most evident among immigrants, who seek out opportunities for community and security with others of like mind and language. The Apostle Peter addressed his first letter to aliens living in strange lands and encouraged them to find their new home among God's chosen people.

Churches have always served as social centers. For my farm-raised parents, their village churches were the only social center available. In the 1950s, migrants from center cities to the suburbs sought out congregations to fill their personal social needs, and new churches blossomed. Millennials today think they satisfy that need through the use social media. Most of them see churches as irrelevant.

The human need to feel different from and superior to others should not be a factor in church life. But it is, and status can be powerful in selecting a church. Early in the 20th century, Pentecostals were looked at as low-class "holy rollers." But as they became more middle-class, they toned down their exuberance and became more accessible. I can recall discussions with Lutherans who congratulated themselves on being different from (and superior to) Baptists.

The fifth need is for self-actualization. What that means is hard to define in business motivation, but it should be clear for churches. We can focus on helping participants grow closer to God. Only churches that appeal to self-actualization needs will do well in the future. Raised on evolutionary theory, many in the newest generations no longer know who they are and why they are here. Their suicide rate is rising. The biblical message has the answer. But it will have to be presented more directly and winsomely in ways that call for a response.

Traditional church cultures developed to address basic needs that are no longer compelling for most Americans. To be effective, churches will have to clarify their purpose and work out new and different church cultures.

What needs seem to drive most of the people that participate in your congregation?

The Spirit Works Toward Self-Actualization

The whole field of motivational psychology was pioneered by Abraham Maslow. His hierarchy of needs is so well known that I treat it as the classical hierarchy. The first four priorities are to satisfy bodily needs, security needs, affiliation needs and status needs. The fifth, the need for self-actualization, is the least explored and the hardest to talk about in business motivation. It makes a lot of sense in the spiritual motivation of Christians.

As happens to prominent people, Maslow's name is invoked by a David Sze in a *Wellness* magazine article of July 21, 2015. Sze was evidently thinking of the *Seven Habits of Effective People* by Stephen Covey, for a while the top selling book in business coaching. Sze used Maslow's name to describe "The Twelve Characteristics of a Self-Actualized Person."

Self-Actualization has become a key concept for "humanistic" psychology aimed at helping men and women become more of what they want to be. An underlying theme is "do what is best for yourself." Humanistic counseling often produces of a lot of divorces as the counselees are encouraged to break free from constraints so they can get all that they deserve.

As I was reading David Sze's list of the 12 characteristics of a self-actualized person, I realized how parallel they are to what happens when the Holy Spirit grows a believer to a higher level of faith. As I list the 12 characteristics, think about where the power comes from to change from where you are to where you want to be. Or for believers, to where God wishes you to be.

*

Self-actualized people: 1) Embrace the unknown and the ambiguous, 2) Accept themselves, together with their flaws, 3) Prioritize and enjoy the journey, not just the destination, 4) Are inherently unconventional, they do not seek to shock or disturb, 5) Are motivated by growth, not by satisfaction of needs, 6) Have purpose, 7) Are not troubled by the small things, 8) Are grateful, 9) Share deep relationships with a few, but also feel identification and affection towards the entire human race, 10) Are humble, 11) Resist enculturation, and 12) Are not perfect.

I could preach on the Spirit at work advancing each of these qualities in a 12-part series.

David Sze must be a Christian because otherwise he wouldn't be conscious of the many characteristics that are foreign to those who stay in their natural condition and do not experience the new life in Christ. Many even remain foreign to believers who stay stuck in Stages Two and Three of faith development.

It takes Spirit-changed believers to be motivated by growth, not by the satisfaction of needs, to be humble, to be grateful and not troubled by small things, to have affection towards the whole human race, to confess they are not perfect, to resist enculteration. Even awareness of that last characteristic is something only Christian churches talk about.

There is a long line of preachers who assume that if they just list human ideals and connect them with Christian behavior, their followers will somehow achieve them—on their own. That might change behavior of passive Christians for a few days. But it is not going to create a desire to embrace the journey of the ambiguous, to be unconventional, to move beyond the satisfaction of needs, to share a deep relationship with a few.

Stay with the thought of relationships. It does not come naturally to humans to "submit to one another out of reverence for Christ." Some want to focus on how unfair it is to women that Paul writes, "Wives, submit to your husband as to the Lord." But that is just a sub-point. His major theme is for wives, husbands, children and slaves to submit to one another, because that is what those under the power of the Spirit will be convicted to do out of reverence to Christ.

Most of what even Christian motivational preaching tries to do does not actually change much behavior. Lasting change happens only when the Spirit moves God's people to new behaviors by changing hearts, by changing inner motivations. Then they can

We Knew Who We Are and Why We're Here

I was waiting at our local Conrads Tire and Auto for a new set of tires to be installed. On the magazine table in the waiting room I saw a hard-covered book on the history of the 30-store chain. It was started after the War by Joan and Ed Conrad. They were and are a staunch Irish Catholic family. They and their kids went to Catholic schools I recognized from the old neighborhood. Their story brought to mind a staunch Irish Catholic neighbor of ours. Their family's kids and ours played a lot together. Daughter of a classic Irish Catholic family, I admire this Mom of seven children. She did and does go to mass every morning.

As I reminisced, I thought, We knew who we are and why we're here. We are created by God to worship him and serve others.

Back then both Catholic and Lutheran church bodies had strong institutions, especially with grade schools, high schools and universities. Those institutions are in retreat. The Catholic bishop of Cleveland closed or merged 50 parishes in 2009. In the Cleveland area we lost four Lutheran grade schools in the past ten years, and the city congregations still remaining are barely hanging on.

For many observers, American society was at its peak in the decades after World War II. Almost everybody would agree that now our society is falling apart, and we anxiously look for leaders who will pull us back together.
*

In his book *The Fractured Republic* Yuval Levin discusses the vital role of mediating institutions in a society. They mediated between individuals and governments. Chief among these were churches that provided valuable community services and neighborhood cohesion. With their decline, families look more to governments to solve their problems and have gotten more dependent on them. Government bureaucracies get bigger. The number of dysfunctional families is increasing. Almost everybody in this country feels strongly that something has to be done.

How many children and adults today know with strong conviction that they are created by God to worship him and serve others? How many have any answer at all to the fundamental life question, Who am I and why am I here? For several generations our public schools have been forced to teach our country's apparent theology that there is no God and we are just products of evolution with no purpose to our living and no reason for character development.

Churches have a fundament role in a healthy society. Through forces nobody could control, the old-line churches are in decline. Thank God there are new church movements emerging that preach and teach the biblical understanding of who we are before God and what he wants us to do with our lives.

More than buildings and organizations, institutions involved role expectations and social interactions. The old church institutions provided what sociologist Peter Berger calls the "sacred canopy" for living. From birth on we experienced an integrated understanding of God and our roles in family, church and work. It was impressed on us in Sunday school, church grade schools, church high schools as well as church universities. Spend twenty years in those church and school institutions and you knew who you are and why you are here. But that life was full of "shoulds," and guilt did provided a lot of motivation to behave as expected.

Living under this sacred canopy over church and society provided meaningful and rewarding lives for many generations of Christians over the centuries. We learned valuable life-time habits, like praying and going to church on Sundays. Most lived out a Confirmed Life in God, with what I have described (Blog 20) as passive convictions or Stage 3 faith. But when institutions crumble, the habits they ingrained start disappearing, too, along with the people who no longer grew up with them.

The church leadership challenge now is to help participants encounter the Spirit who can move them to Stage 4 Convicted Life in God, in which they confident of who they are and why they're here.

Did you grow up when church institutions were still strong? What did you think of your experiences?

The Spirit Arouses God-pleasing Feelings

When I was leading a group on a tour of Israel, we went out on the Sea of Galilee in a tourist boat. We could see many of the special places where Jesus taught and ministered. The operator then played a recording of "How Great Though Art" at a high volume. We all sang the three verses—with more and more gusto. In that setting among believers I knew, our emotions overflowed. The experience blew me away. We were filled with the Spirit and special awe, joy, and unity.

The Spirit works through trigger events. He shapes our response to situations we associate with God. The feeling of awe was aroused from seeing where God walked in the person of Jesus. The feeling of joy came singing a favorite hymn. The feeling of unity came from a special sense of fellowship with other believers we knew. There was a fourth trigger. The boat was rocking in the water, a mildly unsettling experience. The Spirit often does his best work when we are off balance from our usual routines.

How do we know it was the Spirit moving? For us it was in the setting where the Father's love and Christ's grace were evident from Bible stories that happened where we were. Does it work that way with others? I don't know. But I am certain this was the Spirit moving to shape our feelings.

What kind of feelings should we look for?
*
Paul presents the sort of feelings the Spirit produces when he listed the Spirit's fruit: love, joy, peace, patience, kindness, goodness, faithfulness, gentleness and self-control.

Luther describes the Spirit's work as *calling, enlightening, sanctifying* and *keeping* me in the faith. Look for stories of how individuals today experienced a *calling* to a specific ministry, or when they received a *new insight* into the ways of God. I believe being *sanctified*, or set apart, by the Spirit amounts to growing into the motivations and behaviors that Jesus Christ exemplified in his loving outreach to others, the joy he emphasized in his parables, the patience with his followers.

Luther has a second list for the Spirit's work in fellowships of believers, that is, in churches. It is the same functions with the addition of "gathering." This function can provide plenty of stories today of how individuals are gathered into any kind of organized or informal Christian fellowship. What feelings were involved from being in this new relationship? Did the Spirit have anything to do with that?

John Tish is a leader of our Repair Mission teams. Several times a year over a Friday and Saturday we go south about 120 miles to do small house repair projects in the area of Caldwell, Ohio, in the foothills of the Appalachians. He had heard about the work done by HARP, an agency to Help Appalachian Rural People. On his own he drove there to see what was happening, and the coordinator sent him out to appraise projects.

He was appalled by the living conditions he saw among the poor who could get no help. He became part of the next team that went. On a recent trip he thought of a way to engage others from church, and took leadership to make it happen. What feelings were involved? He reports empathy, gratitude for his blessings, a sense of calling to lead this ministry. Do you think the Spirit was involved?

Kevin Park is the church member who designed and minted the two-sided coin described in the blog 17 "Look on the Other Side of the Coin." In the last 15 years he has distributed 150,000 of them. When the conviction came that he should personally make this coin, he describes hearing a rushing sound like snow falling from tree. It was clear to him that he had been called to this ministry.

Have you experienced a call to do some kind of service to others?

Look on The Other Side of the Coin

Kevin Park is a member of our church who designed and by now has distributed 150,000 grace and mercy coins. One side has cross and the words "Mercy is when God spares you what you deserve." The other side has a dove and the words "Grace is when God gives you what you don't deserve." It's a great evangelism tool.

The first side's cross represents Christ. The other side's dove is for the Holy Spirit. *Mercy* is the proper word for the forgiveness God gives us through Christ's redemption. The Bible word is *charis* for the gift given, which we call grace. A second kind of grace is called *charisma*, the gift received. This is always associated with the Holy Spirit. One form is the special energy he gives to do specific ministries (1 Corinthians 12). The other is the higher gifts of love, faith and hope (12:31) and other fruit the Spirit produces in believers, like joy and patience.

The Reformation was all about mercy and assurance of eternal life. For that purpose we were taught to look toward what Christ had accomplished on the cross. When Paul wrote about the church life of his congregations, he actually focused more on the other side of the coin, what the Holy Spirit was currently doing. He used the phrase "in Christ" 81 times. He explained "by the Spirit" 143 times.

So which is it?

*

A breakthrough discovery for me from the work of Lewis Smedes was to recognize how for the same function Paul used Christ in one passage and the Spirit in a different one. Here are several of a total of 13 pairings: We are righteous in Crist; we are righteous in the Holy Spirit. We have life through Christ; we have life through the Spirit. We have hope grounded in Christ; we have hope grounded in the power of the Spirit. He used both sides of the coin interchangeably.

A simple observation will clarify why we do better to focus now on the Spirit, the dove side of the coin. In the Apostle's Creed we confess that Jesus Christ "ascended into heaven, where he sits at the right hand of God the Father and will come again to judge the living and the dead."

41

So where is Christ now? We believe he is in heaven in a position of authority with his Father.

Jesus himself taught his followers that his Father will send the Spirit of truth, the Advocate, to be with them and in them. This Advocate will "remind you of everything I (Jesus) have taught you." Doctrinal language uses the title Holy Spirit. Mostly in Scriptures this Third Person of the Trinity is named simply "the Spirit." I can defend identifying him as Christ's Spirit.

Imagine the Spirit as the dove who flew down from above and sat on Jesus' shoulder at his baptism. In my life I envision him whispering into my ear, advocating godly thoughts and intentions and guiding me through the day.

Think of the Spirit at work changing human spirits, as Jesus taught Nicodemus. The Spirit is transforming us in supernatural ways that simple human counseling cannot. The Spirit generates the passion to share the Gospel with others and to learn new ways to do so more effectively

Jesus explained to Nicodemus that the Spirit is a wind whose direction cannot be predicted. He brings winds of change into church life. The Reformation was such an unpredictable change. We are witnessing big changes now happening in the understanding and effective ministry practices of many churches in North America.

For traditional churches, will this unpredictable movement of the Spirit be welcomed or resisted? Leaders of institutionalized churches are prone to resist this part of the Spirit's work. Pray that the Spirit opens their hearts and minds to try innovative ministries.

Would you be willing to consider the Holy Spirit as Christ's Spirit and advocate?

Churches Running Almost on Empty

The three biblical symbols for the Spirit at work are the dove who sat on Jesus' shoulder at his baptism, and the tongues of fire and rushing wind at Pentecost. Jesus described the wind as unpredictable. Consider the following interpretation of what those symbols represented.

The tongues of *fire* suggest energy, the kind associated with heavy work that flushes the face and increases the heart beat, like being on fire for the Lord. The unpredictable *wind* is the Spirit bringing unexpected changes into lives and relationship.

I think of the Spirit as a *dove* sitting on my shoulder whispering godly thoughts as my day goes on. I do have ongoing conversation about what to do a specific situation, especially whether to speak my mind or deny myself. I identify many tempting thoughts as coming from the Enemy whispering into my other ear. I see these thoughts reflecting what Luther described as daily washing away our old nature and letting the new person come forth—the process of the Spirit changing me little by little, with the occasional "a-ha" insight that changes my thinking and reactions.

Many call this conversational prayer, as distinct from formal prayer. They usually consider conversational prayer to be the essence of the prayer relationship with God. It approaches what Paul from his experience described as "Be joyful always, pray continually, give thanks in all circumstances." (1 Thessalonians 5:16). The book I have written a book on that distinction and how individuals experience it is *How the Spirit Shapes Prayer* (2017).
*

Let's follow Luther and distinguish between the Spirit energizing individuals and churches. Pastoral work involves episodes of coming alongside believers going through personal changes and growing in their trust and relationship to God. The Spirit is at work. But it also involves recognizing so many who are, in shorthand, C and E Christians, reflecting almost no Spiritual life and energy.

To be Lutheran is to recognize that both kinds will be in heaven. Meanwhile the leadership challenge is to help them find more of the abundant life here that Jesus promised and the Spirit delivers. Promoting this Spiritual growth amounts to a mission even without reaching new people.

We can certainly speak of the Spiritual life or energy of congregations. It is easier to spot the absence of Spirit influence when the same people do the same things the same way year after year. They appear to be relying on human energy that over time is getting weaker in a downward spiral. They act like a social club organized for their mutual benefit with a veneer of holy words. Their gas tank of Spiritual energy is running almost on empty. Their death may be long and lingering, but most communities have the skeletal remains of institutionalized churches that died. God nowhere promises long life to church fellowship that don't seek the Spirit.

Use the same markers of energy and change to recognize congregations where the Spirit is welcomed and at work. Look for an organized prayer life. The worship is engaging with a lot of variety. They have a lot of members doing a range of ministries and missions for others, and probably teach spiritual gift administration. They are welcoming too others attracted by their community reputation. There usually are innovations going on in this or that program. They emphasize individual growth and journey. Coincidentally they also often have numeric growth. In sum, their Spiritual gas tank seems full and there is a sense of excitement for the years ahead.

If you are in a church with an almost empty energy tank, start by praying the Father to send his Spirit, look for opportunities to change something, and seek the Spirit's guidance.

How Paul Recognized the Spirit

The Apostle Paul was an organizational genius. In today's terms he was a world-class entrepreneur, planting and developing dozens of congregations of a brand new religion throughout the Roman world.

Paul was a keen observer of human nature and emotions. After he was blinded on the way to Damascus, Ananias came to him, and we read that he was full of the Holy Spirit and could see again.

He observed how the earliest churches were strengthened and encouraged by the Holy Spirit. On the way to Iconium he and other disciples were "filled with joy and with the Holy Spirit." What do you think each of those experiences felt like? Imagine what it is like to see again, and how it feels to be filled with joy and to witness congregations get encouraged.

My point is that—between his conversion about 36 A.D. and his death thirty years later—he recognized thousands of incidents when the Spirit changed the lives of people around him just as the Spirit dramatically changed his own life. Each was a story of personal change that happened through encounters with the Gospel message.

Above all, Paul was what we would call today a very high-level analyst.
*

He could examine "data" of his experiences and observations, and then write up a report that made sense and interpreted what was happening to the people he was writing to. We have learned to read these as generalizations that teach doctrine. I think it better to see those as interpretations of what the readers were experiencing—where they were getting it right and where they were going astray. Everybody he wrote to personally knew how the Spirit had changed their lives.

 Probably the first epistle he wrote was to the Galatians. He reminds them that God sent the Spirit into their hearts. We can assume each could remember when, where and how that happened.

Towards the end of the report, Paul encourages them to live by and keep in step with the Spirit, the Spirit who has been at work producing new life in them, where love, joy, peace, patience are growing. Later letters have other variations on these descriptions of the motivating feelings the Spirit produces when he enters into the hearts of believers. Paul is continually encouraging these readers, most of whom he knew, to keep growing and abounding in their new motivations.

These insights came from studying Gordon F. Fee's thick book *God's Empowering Presence*, his detailed study of the 143 references to the Spirit in Paul's writings. Fee writes, "It is certain that the Pauline churches were "charismatic" in the sense that a dynamic presence of the Spirit was manifested in their gatherings. And even where power means that believers apprehend and live out the love of Christ in a greater way, Paul recognizes here a miraculous work of the Spirit that will be *evidenced* by the way renewed people behave toward one another.

"It is this dynamic, evidential dimension of life in the Spirit that probably more than anything else separates believers in later church history from those in the Pauline churches. Whatever else, the Spirit was *experienced* in the Pauline churches; he was not merely a matter of creedal assent." (824)

The phrase "filled with the Holy Spirit" for Paul means that somebody looked and felt empowered to do what Paul witnessed. Paul's protégé and traveling companion was Luke, who uses his mentor's favorite phrase in writing his Gospel and Book of Acts.

There was a time my personal career when I had the title "Analyst." My Ph.D. training in Organizational Behavior is great preparation to be a consultant as well as a professor. Observe a problematic situation, figure out what's going wrong and recommend courses of action to remedy it.

This project is my report on what's wrong with mainline churches and how to fix it. We do believe the Spirit is still working today. Recognize when and where. Look for someone (yourself?) who recently felt empowered by the Spirit in interaction with others. Then give witness.

Can you give witness to evidence that the Spirit is still working today?

Do Supernatural Miracles Really Happen?

By the late 1990s, I had growing curiosity about whether miracles really do happen today. If so, our Calvinist and Lutheran heritage is wrong in teaching that miracles happened only in Bible times. If so, prayer for healing opens a new type of ministry. If so, university elites are missing a whole dimension of the world around us. If so, the personal worldviews of traditional church pastors and leaders are unnecessarily limiting their understanding of what God can do in this world. If so, the Holy Spirit can indeed change our human spirit. (Blog 10))

Let Lutheran seminary professor Loren Halverson describe the implications as he explains the epistemological revolution going on in the late 20th century:
*

> This cultural revolution (toward appreciating the supernatural) suggests a shift in one's mode of being and doing that so radically reverses, upsets, and disorients that it amounts to a conversion or a passage through Alice's mirror. In it the same reality is seen, the same data observed, but everything is different, perhaps even opposite, and new conclusions and actions result. The empirical and experiential are the same, but reviewed with new eyes. I believe that the change has more to do with the vision than analysis, serendipity than calculation, the Holy Spirit than prescribed ritual and dogma.

Here are some of my personal observations and discoveries during the years when I was looking for evidence of an extraordinary event for which there is no natural explanation. There is no scientifically irrefutable evidence, and never will be to the highest scientific standards.   But for me the issue is resolved. Extraordinary events for which there is no natural explanation do occur—but not very often.

For several years once a month I did Sunday evening prayer-for-healing services, under the tutelage of an elderly Presbyterian pastor who for years had been doing healing services in his congregation. What is very clear to me is that I do not have what Paul calls the gift of healing.

In the 1990s after his own healing, physician Paul Prather went on a search for evidence of unexplainable bodily healings. After four Benny Hinn rallies he interviewed about 300 people who thought they had been healed. In his educated opinion the vast majority were not real. But he saw five to ten he did believe were supernaturally restored to heath.

I learned about the Roman Catholic beatification process for declaring someone a saint. A necessary step is having a panel of practicing university physicians read through medical records on two healings attributed to the prayers of the candidate proposed for beatification. Only when they see evidence for a healing that has no possible alternate explanation do they refer the candidate on for consideration by the pope. To me that is convincing.

I joined a pastoral colleague on a teaching mission accompanying the ministry of Uma Ukpai, Miracle Worker in Abakaliki, Nigeria. When the Miracle Worker called out for people who wanted healing of a specific sort, 50-100 in the audience would fall down on the ground and do a corkscrew twisting. The American physician sitting next to me explained the neurological connection associated with that twisting. But there was no possible way of verifying whether the disease had been cured in anyone.

The most convincing testimonies are those gathered by Eric Metaxas in his book *Miracles: What They Are, Why They Happen, and How They Can Change Your Life* (2014). He told the stories only of those whom he personally knew. One was a fellow Lutheran pastor. I heard him tell his story of a crippling disease that took him to a Benny Hinn rally. He was fully healed, and now does a very active healing ministry.

The closest I came to witnessing a miraculous healing involved a teen at our church who experienced a brain aneurism on a Saturday evening. When her mother took her to the emergency room, the doctors said that even if she survived the night she would not be able to walk or talk. At 11:00 am, after the 9:45 Sunday service, we gathered about fifty worshipers in a big circle and prayed for her healing. We got word back in the afternoon that at 11:00 am she woke up and talked and walked.

Have you experienced or witnessed a miracle in your life, defined as an extraordinary event for which there is no natural explanation?

How I Discovered I Am a Mystic. You May Be, Too

As I drive around town, I listen to university lectures on a c from The Great Courses. The most recent was Mystical Traditions, taught by Professor Luke Johnson from Emory University. While listening I discovered I am a mystic.

I used to have zero interest in mysticism. It was soft-headed thinking and much like poetry. Usually I skip over poetry when I am reading something. I want rational description, as systematic as possible. Eventually I figured out Luke Johnson's definition of mysticism. It is "encounters with the divine." That I can get excited about, since I have focused for years now on how believers experience God.

In his several millennia overview, Johnson got to the 18th century Pietist movement in Germany, roughly parallel to Puritanism in England. Those pastors and church leaders reacted against the scholasticism prevalent in Lutheran universities and among preachers of that time.   Naturally the university teachers reacted against that movement.
*

Usually in a contest between hard headed and soft headed, the rational hard heads win out, especially in academic discussions of theology and ministry. They heaped scorn on the Pietists, who indeed actually kept church life alive in the sterile age of Enlightenment.

The most popular writing was, in Latin, *Pia Desideria* by P. J. Spener, which is the source of the name Pietists. An English translation would be Fervent Yearnings. He was calling for renewal movement within the Lutheran churches of his day.

He called for making sure those in the office of ministry are themselves truly Christians. He wanted congregational life to revolve around the Word, which should be studied in small groups. In what we would call evangelism, he called for approaching the erring (the unchurched) by clarifying that our truth is based on the simple teachings of Jesus and making clear that they see we are acting out of a heart-felt love toward them. Over all, "It is not enough that we hear the Word with our outward ear, but we must let it penetrate our heart, so that we may hear the Holy Spirit speak there."

In his overview of mysticism, when Luke Johnson got to the 19th century, he highlighted the *Erweckungbewegung*, the Awakening Movement in Germany. That was part of the surge of nationalism after the collapse of Napoleon's empire. Rediscovering Luther and Bach was part of that movement.

What I found so interesting is that my church body, The Lutheran Church—Missouri Synod, was a product of that Awakening Movement. The leader of it in Dresden led an 800-member colony of Saxons to St. Louis in 1839. C.F.W. Walther soon became their leader. He reveled in the newly re-discovered Luther and his writings.

Even though leaders of our Synod today don't want to acknowledge it, Walther and other early leaders in that German-speaking colony were Pietists. I demonstrated that in an article based on Luther's writings, but I couldn't get it published in our seminary journals.

In 1862 the second president of our synod, Heinrich Schwan, chastised his fellow pastors for being too legalistic. He described evangelistic (Gospel-based) church practices and gave examples of them over-against legalistic (Law-based) practices. He traced their present situation to "the natural tendency of the old Adam and our origin in pietistic circles."

All church movements have an exciting beginning, but then get simplified to living by simplistic rules and rituals. Few faculty and pastors in the 20th century were interested in the beginnings of Pietism, especially after they lost the ability to read German. What most heard is that Pietists were legalistic, and they did not want any of that in their modern church.

So it turns out I am a mystic. If you have had "encounters with the divine," you are, too.

Look for the Present Spirit to Balance Biblical Memory

John Shea is a popular storyteller among Roman Catholics. He is also a profound non-academic theologian. His main book is *An Experience Named Spirit*. He is a good guide to how the Spirit is experienced in life. Thus he can help us learn how to better recognize the Spirit at work around us.

He urges us to recognize the SPIRIT in encounters that become STORIES. There are two kinds: those that happened a long time ago in *MEMORY* and those that are fresh encounters. The stories most helpful identify the TRIGGER EVENTS.

Shea starts with this welcome assumption: "The essence of Christian faith is a living relationship with God, a relationship which was inaugurated by Jesus of Nazareth and which is presently available through his Spirit as it suffuses and transforms the lives of his followers."

To verify that new encounters are of the Spirit, he highlights three features expected by Paul. Was the present activity attributed to the inspiration of the Spirit in continuity with the founding gospel tradition, did it manifest love, and was it for the benefit of others?

"In 'the time of its happening' a given experience may have religious potential. But this potential will only be actualized 'over time' through a retelling process. It is important that the telling of the experience be in story form. Story telling has a power of involvement and appreciation that the mere noting of patterns or talking about experiences analytically does not have."

*

John Shea challenges us to identify the triggers that bring religiously significant experiences.

"Church and Tradition have an enshrined set of triggers. Through hearing the story of Jesus, participating in the sacraments, attending Mass, meditating, engaging in certain prayer practices people enter explicitly in to their relationship to God. But a second and more extensive set of triggers are the multiple life situations in which people find themselves. In situations of sickness and vitality, of questing for truth and struggling for justice, of loving and reconciling, of pondering the vastness of space and of traveling the inner endless journey of the psyche, people come upon the reality of God. In fact, that seems to be the more traveled path to religious awareness today.

"The trigger power of the creations of the Christian tradition is seriously questioned now. The presence that people used to find in the dark back of Gothic churches they now claim they find in the bright lights of the secular world. Our interests are in bringing these two sets of triggers together."

Story-teller John Shea warns what happens when we do not tell stories of fresh experiences. "When we retain the message of the King but lose the feel for his presence, the passion of religious mission turns to dull obligation." (47) Without being balanced with fresh experiences religious traditions usually generate into rationalistic theology, a formal morality and a religious cult. Sometimes a religion which is nothing more has ceased to exist.

Shea explains that his categories of current Spirit and backward-looking Memory defy neat categories. Christian history is a sprawling chronical of a people energized by their living relationship to God who are creating multiple responses to their diverse environments.

I commend John Shea's observation that Spirit and Memory are critical correctives. "In the excesses and pretensions of the Spirit we look to the Memory of Jesus for direction and perspective. But when Memory threatens to alienate us from the depth of the present, we look to the Spirit to bring us life."

Traditional churches are disappearing into Memory. We definitely now need to recognize more experiences of the current Spirit at work.

Chapter 4

Discipled by the Spirit

Discipleship is a key concept for current Protestants. But in my experience discipleship opportunities do not draw much attention. That's because it is a "should" action, usually appealing to guilt. The Spirit grows disciples by shaping their motivations to experience more of what God offers and thus become closer to him.

Blogs

12. Growing into a Free, Cheerful, Glad and Loving Heart

18 Stuck at Stage 2, Staying at Stage 3

24. Growing Closer to God Is Like Peak Performance by Athletes

30. Have You Hit the "Wall" Yet?

36. How's Your Spiritual Journey?

42. Moving From Growing in Christ, to Close to Christ, to Christ-Centered

48. What is Your Spiritual Temperament?

Growing Into Free, Cheerful, Glad and Loving Hearts

"When the Spirit comes, he makes a pure, free, cheerful, glad and loving heart—a conscience made righteous by grace, seeking no reward, fearing no punishment, doing everything with joy."

These are the words of Martin Luther in a sermon he preached in 1521. The Spirit was very much in the center of his thinking in those early years of the Reformation. He was not a systematic theologian. But what he intuited in this off-hand comment happens to fit the stages of faith recognized in modern developmental psychology.

Luther described three kinds of conscience, which are three stages of faith. A churchyard conscience concentrates on getting the external rules of church life right. A nave (pew section) conscience characterizes those who are living faithfully but out of guilt with no joy. Progressing forward, those who are living with a heart changed by the Spirit have a chancel-conscience. "Conscience" in classical theology describes what I call motivation.

*

Stage One in the developmental psychology of faith development is the literal-mindedness of a toddler. Stage two focuses on fairness and learning the rules. Stage Three is belief in and living according to what the church teaches—passive faith. Stage Four is Convicted Life in God. Luther's chancel faith is what I would call the fifth stage of Living Close to God. A reasonable goal in ministry is to help believers learn to live Close to God. This stage is what the Apostle Paul described when he urged the Thessalonians to "be joyful always; pray continually, give thanks in all circumstances."

All five stages represent a Christian faith that brings eternal life. The first stage is that of a toddler who thinks in literal terms and cannot distinguish a heavenly Father from earthly fathers. Jesus taught that unless you have the faith of a child you cannot enter the kingdom of God. Paul taught that all who call on the name of Jesus Christ will have life eternal life. We can add, whatever stage of faith they are in.

For most believers over the centuries of the Christian era, living in this world was to have lots of pain and insecurity. Just think, Luther and Calvin didn't even have aspirin. Seeking better life in the *next* world was a very strong motivator. In contrast current life in America is very comfortable for most. Current motivators have to do with finding a better life in *this* world—daily living with more meaning and more love, joy and peace *now*.

Daily living is where the Third Person of the Trinity operates. The Second, Jesus Christ, ascended into heaven where he sits at the right hand of the First Person, God the Father, to return only at the final judgment. The Father and the Son send the Holy Spirit to be their advocates to unbelievers but especially to those who say Jesus is Lord, as Paul writes. Using the image of the dove at Jesus' baptism, I think of the Spirit sitting as a dove on my shoulder whispering godly thoughts as my day goes along. It is the Spirit who stimulates our faith to grow.

Our challenge as traditional Christians in the 21st century is to present the Good News as it applies to living daily life *now*, not just in the *next* world. The Gospel of eternal salvation in Jesus Christ by grace remains basic. The second part of the Good News is what Paul calls "spiritual gifts," flowing from the grace gifts of the Spirit that God sends to work in our hearts now. Enjoying the fruit of the Spirit here and now amounts to recovering what has become the forgotten Gospel.

The biblical word for "save" can also be translated "heal." The ultimate healing is in heaven. But healing in the kingdom of God starts now, especially spiritual healing of the unfulfilling life so many have who are far from God.

Are you willing to advocate the forgotten Gospel appropriate for those in the 21st century living far from God?

Stuck at Stage Two, Staying on Stage 3

I was teaching a class of about 30 lay pastors. On the second day, one raised his hand and asked whether you could smoke and still be a Christian. I stopped what we were doing and led a long discussion on being saved by grace, not by works that you do or don't do. The next day I asked this same individual, "So can you smoke and still be a Christian?" His answer? No, that's not possible.

What was that all about? Was I such a bad teacher? I can understand better now after working with insights from developmental psychologist James Fowler. He distinguishes stages of faith development. The first stage is that of a small child who cannot distinguish the heavenly Father from a physical father. The second is typical of kids, often in middle school, whose approach to life revolves around fairness. The third is, "I believe what my church teaches." The fourth is having personal convictions: "This is what I personally believe."

These stages are easiest to spot as children grow. But they can also be seen in adults who stay stuck at an earlier stage.
*

Many adults want to approach God in terms of fairness— Because I have tried to live a good life, God will be good to me. I remember a survey of Lutheran adults that showed half think they will go to heaven because of the good life they lived here. Over decades of church life, how could they miss the distinctive Lutheran teaching of grace? The answer, I think, is that, like the adult lay pastor, their brains are stuck at a level-two development stage. Most little children grow out of the earliest stages as their brains develop. But many adults never get beyond stage-two thinking that you have to earn what you get. Yet because of his grace, God loves them still.

Traditional churches emphasize stage-three faith development by teaching children the head-knowledge of the doctrinal truths of their faith. We call this Confirmation. Then they are expected to live the rest of their lives faithful to this **Confirmed Life in God**. Many did and do. Even though the faith of many remains shallow, God's kingdom has borne much fruit in such church life.

I want to advocate two more stages of faith development for believers whom God has blessed with the capability to seek to develop further in their relationship with him. Stage Four is a faith that has been tested in experience and moves into deeper heart conviction. Believers with such faith move beyond passive church life to energetically reach out and serve others. We can call this stage **Convicted Life in God**.

I propose yet a fifth stage of faith development. It is for those blessed with the capability to reflect on their thoughts and feelings as they go through life. This stage is for believers who are being led to purposely seek more of the life-enhancing qualities like love, joy and peace that the Holy Spirit wants to produce in the daily lives of God's people. I would name this the stage of **Close to God**.

My goal in sharing these thoughts and insights is to promote discussion with believers about their discoveries and desires as they experience their Christian walk. Realistically these will be believers in or moving toward Stage 4, Convicted Life in God. Those most interested in future discussions I am offering will be among believers ready for Stage 5 of Close to God.

Consider also that congregations where most stay stuck at Stage 3 are probably not going to survive long in our current American culture.

What stage of faith do you think you are at now? What stage of faith would you like to grow into? Keep in mind that most people cannot recognize a stage higher than the one ahead of them.

Growing Closer to God
Is Like Peak Performance by Athletes

Over my years of membership in the American Psychological Association, I watched my division of industrial and organizational psychology spin off a new specialty called sports psychology. Those psychologists focus on helping athletes to reach peak performance. They explore mental practices an athlete can do to squeeze out a little more speed or increase endurance by a few minutes.

The early Christian church had its version of top athletes, superior practitioners of Christian spirituality. After Christianity got absorbed into the Roman Empire, it acquired many members with questionable motivations. Those who considered themselves real Christians sought a way to show commitment.

*

You have to understand the setting. They came along after believers at the turn into the fourth century experienced the worst persecution in the first two-and-a-half centuries of Christian history. Of those martyrs not cruelly put to death, many walked around with missing limbs or bore bodily evidence of the consequences for not recognizing the emperor as a "son of God," the title first given to Caesar Augustus by the Roman Senate. Such martyrdom for the cause impressed many observers and contributed to the explosive growth of Christianity in the fourth century.

With that option gone after Christianity was legitimatized, some believers sought other ways to demonstrate "peak performance." They went out into the desert to live as hermits. Bishop Athanasius, for whom the Athanasian Creed was named, wrote the biography of Antony of Egypt, the hermit who first gained public recognition. Antony's story raised up many others who became hermits to be closer to God.

I share this historical observation to raise the question: where should we look today for Christians seeking to be "close to God"?

In medieval times, the monks and clergy were recognized as closer to God than everyone else, the laity. Luther and Calvin recovered Paul's teaching that all are ministers. Getting closer to God is an opportunity open to all believers, whether or not they pursue it.

The advent of 20th century stage theory of faith development clarifies what the peak performance of getting closer to God looks like and how to get there. I have described Stage 5 Faith as that consciousness of being close to God and continuing to grow in what the Spirit produces: love, joy, peace, patience and similar qualities.

Unlike superior athletes today who crave attention and bragging rights (as well as higher pay), the peak performance of believers is only possible through a humbling experience. On their own, believers will never experience peak-satisfying levels of love, joy, and peace. That level only happens to believers when the Spirit enters and changes their hearts. The Spirit has to move us to more comprehensive love, joy and peace—closer to God.

Like a sports psychologist, I can give advice on practices that will more readily bring about Stage 5 living. These disciplines have been known through centuries of church life. I have summarized them in the six practices for GROWTH in the Spirit: **G**o to God in worship and prayer, **R**eceive God's word for you, **O**pt for self-denial, give **W**itness to your experiences, **T**rust God in a new venture, and **H**umble yourself before God.

Recognize that most of the growth in our spirituality is driven by the Holy Spirit. What we can do on our own is keep ourselves where the Spirit can most readily work in us, in his workplace of believers gathered around the Word.

Like little Zacchaeus, we can figuratively climb a tree so we can better recognize the Spirit and then keep ourselves where he can work on us. Like Jesus who spotted Zachaeus up in the tree and invited him down for a time of meal-fellowship, we can let the Spirit draw us into closer fellowship with him. This is God's Spirit, the Spirit of Christ with us today, the Spirit sent by the Father and Son to be their advocate for more godly and abundant living here and now.

Would you like to grow closer to God?

Have You Hit the Wall Yet?

For Janet Hagberg and Robert Guelich each, the wall was a failed marriage that took them by surprise. Successful in everything else they had done, each had to process this new reality. Each came out of it a better person, closer to God.

They describe that process in their book *The Critical Journey: Stages in the Life of Faith* (1989). Add their stages to Luther's intuitive three kinds of conscience (Blog 6). Pioneer developmental psychologist James Fowler's presents five stages. The key two I have renamed "I believe what the church teaches" (Stage 3) and "This is what I believe" (stage 4). Common to all is a similar description of Stages Three and Four. Hagberg and Guelich give their own name to that critical transition. It is hitting "the wall." Luther called it *tentatio,* struggle.

Here is the Hagberg and Guelich description of what can happen when we get on the other side of whatever Wall we personally have run into:

*

"A crisis can knock us off balance, making us afraid, vulnerable and ripe for change. This also happens in our spiritual journey. We have a crisis in our faith that causes us to reconsider. It might frighten us, at least make us vulnerable. If we become bitter or too resistant, we can get stuck. But if we let the change or crisis touch us, if we live with it and embrace it, we are more likely to grow and to move eventually to another stage or spiral in our journey. When we are most vulnerable, we have the best chance to learn and move along the way. In the midst of pain there is promise."

Many believers get stuck in a Stage Two or Three, as I described in Blog 18. Here is what Hagberg and Guelich observe:

"It is easy to mislead people into thinking that they can move themselves to the next stage by just doing the things listed, talking to the right people, or setting their mind to it. Nothing could be further from the truth. The journey of faith is our personal journey, and movement on the journey is the place of mystery, holy ground."

They observe what I personally have observed. Moving on requires the help of others. We can glibly say to read the Word. But we need others beyond the preacher to interpret and reflect its practical meaning personally.

In Luther's Large Catechism explanation of the third article of the creed (I believe in the Holy Spirit), he notes that the next phrase is "the communion of saints." He writes, "Until the last day, the Holy Spirit remains with the holy community of Christian people. Through it (the community) he gathers us, using it to teach and preach the Word. By it he creates and increases sanctification, causing it daily to grow and become strong in the faith and in the fruits of the Spirit."

In the Smalcald Articles, which he personally wrote, Luther describes how the Gospel is communicated through the means of grace. He lists the fifth as "the mutual conversation and consolation of brethren."

It is critical to avoid leaving the impression that believers at earlier stages are somehow inferior. They are simply not enjoying all the benefits available to believers. Moving on happens at the initiative of the Spirit. What all can do is pray Come, Holy Spirit, Come! We can all sing Luther's hymn "Come, Holy Ghost, God and Lord, Be all your graces now outpoured on each believer's mind and heart; Your fervent love to them impart."

I found it interesting to discover that my hero, Danish existentialist philosopher Søren Kierkegaard, mused about the stages of life. He famously described "the leap of faith," based on Abraham's willingness to sacrifice his son Isaac at God's command, as irrational as God's action seemed. That was a Wall experience for him.

Have you encountered a significant Wall in your life?

What's Your Spiritual Journey?

Telling about one's spiritual journey is common in Evangelical communities. It's an invitation to talk about your conversion. But there is no reason why mainline Christians can't do that, too, even though we are usually baptized as infants. I advocate telling about your spiritual journey in terms of how close or far from God you have been over the years of your life.

I invite you to think in terms of the chart below left. It is small. You can reproduce it on a larger sheet of paper. Plot out your personal journey.
*

The vertical line represents how far or close you were at various stages of your life, represented by the horizontal line. What was your God relationship when you were confirmed, if that's your story? For some that is a time of closeness, when the truths they have been taught in catechism class make sense—at an eighth-grade level.

Then comes a time of drifting away during the challenging years of high school. Maybe the drift is further down on the chart during college and young adulthood. Often with young adult responsibilities of marriage and children comes a return to attending church, and that is where you stay with sporadic and passive attendance. The small-dotted line represents the old understanding when the ideal was to stay faithful to your confirmation vows.

If your congregation is well functioning, you get drawn into more fellowship and growth in your relationship with God. Your journey line goes up as the years progress. You are being drawn closer to God. In comparison to your earlier years, where are you now on the chart? This journey is drawn on the chart to the right.

Here is the payoff question. Where do you want to be in the future? Are you going to stay as you are? Or do you want to grow even closer to God?

The chart on the right is the typical journey of a church-attending believer in a mainline congregation What's next for you on your chart? Are you going to stay about where you are now in your relationship with God? In other blogs I have presented five stages of faith. It's the third, fourth and fifth stages I want to highlight. The third is typical of most members in a mainline church—confirmed passive faith. Some are at the fourth stage—convicted active faith an involvement in congregational life. A few make it to the fifth stage of faith and ministry—very close to God.

Movement from third to fourth stage is not something you do on your own. The Holy Spirit has to move you there. Often that comes through a Wall experience when you cannot maintain the life routines you have had, through perhaps a serious illness, or loss of a job, or death of someone close to you. Then spiritual truths you have confessed take on much more meaning. They become convicted faith with more active involvement in serving others. You know who you are in Christ and want to worship God and serve others.

Why would you want to grow beyond Stage 3 of head-oriented confirmed faith? Because then the Spirit can bring about more of his special fruit in your life—his gifts of more love, joy, peace patience and other motivations like that. Who would not want to grow into more of these characteristics?

While the Spirit brings the changes in motivation, you can take action to help that process. You can put yourself in the Spirit's workplace—a fellowship of believers who share God's word and make personal application to their life situations.

You can learn to wait upon the Spirit. You can do GROWTH practices. You can **G**o to God in worship and prayer, **R**ead his Word for you, **O**wn your self-denial, give **W**itness to your Experiences, **T**rust God in a new venture and **H**umble Yourself before God.

These GROWTH practices are presented in blogs 7, 19, 25 and 51.

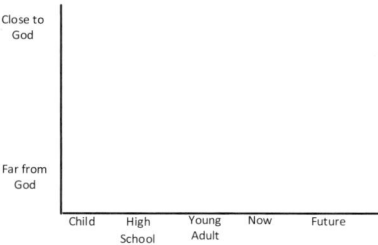

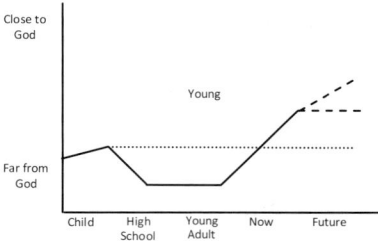

64

Moving from Growing in Christ to Close to Christ, to Christ-Centered

Willow Creek Community Church has been *the* leader of out-reach-oriented Protestant church leaders. They head up a network of such leaders. They also sponsor church growth-oriented research.

George L Hawkins and Cally Parkinson head up REVEAL, which uses research tool and discoveries to help churches better understand spiritual growth in their congregations. Their report of one project is *MOVE: What 1,000 Churches Reveal About Spiritual Growth* (2011). They explored four levels of spirituality among participants in of those congregations. Key is the movement from lower to higher.

Many participants start out Exploring Christ. The movement is from there to Growing in Christ, to Close to Christ, to Christ-centered. Their second, third and fourth levels are similar to third, fourth and fifth stages of faith development I have identified.

The variables were Spiritual Beliefs and Attitudes, Personal Spiritual Practices, Organized Church Activities, and Spiritual Activities with Others. Church leadership received special attention.

Most important is what happens to participants when they move from Growing in Christ (my stage 3) to Christ-Centered (stage 5). The percentage increases for those who report that they love God more than anything else. They are willing to risk everything important in their life and feel more equipped to share their faith. They study the Bible and pray daily for guidance, and they serve others on their own.

The researcher's insight is that spiritual growth is all about movement of the heart. The transformation is toward deeply held convictions that are lived out in practice in a way that becomes integrated with the rest of their life.

They were particularly interested in the roughly twenty percent who reported themselves dissatisfied and stalled. Here is the help they wanted from their church. Initially they wanted to develop a personal relationship with Christ. At the next two levels (Close to Christ and Christ-centered) they wanted to understand the Bible. They also wanted church leaders to model how to grow, and then they wanted to be challenged to grow personally, with a clear pathway to do so.

Out of all the variables, the researchers constructed a measure of spiritual vitality. They distinguished between the apathetic, the introverted, the average and the high energy congregations. Any congregation can work with Reveal to get their score on spiritual vitality and find where they are on this scale from apathetic to high-energy. They concluded that:

- Churches that are high energy concentrate on getting people moving, embedding the Bible in everything they do, creating ownership, and pastoring the local community.

- To get people moving leaders need to make the destination clear, make the spiritual jump-start non-negotiable, and make the senior pastor the champion.

- To embed the Bible in everything, make it the main course of the message, take away the excuses, and model Scripture as the church's foundation.

- To create ownership, empower people to be the church, equip people to succeed, hold people accountable.

- To pastor the local community, set a high bar for serving the church and the community, build a bridge into your local community, and make serving a platform for the Gospel.

- Christ-centered leaders are disarmingly humble, they model a surrendered life, and they focus on growing hearts not on growing attendance.

I would rate the congregation I serve as above average. The question for our leadership team is how important it is to grow to the level of a high-energy congregation. If so, the Reveal studies show what we have to do.

The issue for any congregation is how much spiritual growth is important to them and how much energy they want to put into the tasks. It's not going to happen without forceful leadership.

What's Your Spiritual Temperament?

Did you know that you have a spiritual temperament? This means some activities help you feel closer to God than others things you do. And people have different spiritual temperaments. So if you want to be drawn closer to God spend more time on the spiritual pathways that work best for you.

These are insights from a new branch of psychology associated with the names Myers and Briggs. The Myers-Briggs Personality Inventory is the most-used testing instrument in business human resource management. One familiar distinction from their work is between introverts and extraverts.

I first ran into the insights on spiritual temperaments reading the book *Who You Are Is How You Pray*, by Charles Keating. He applied the Myers and Briggs personality types to members of religious orders to help candidates find the right one. He highlights the view of Ignatius Loyola, founder of the Jesuits, who urged those seeking to be closer to God to try out different approaches and disciplines to find the one that is "sweet" for each. Don't just imitate what someone else does.
*

Do you feel closer to God when you are hiking in nature? Or when you are caring for others? Or when you are alone thinking about God? Or when you are with other believers praising God with high emotions? Or when you are out crusading for peace and justice? Or when you are worshiping in a building with lots of symbols using special rituals? Or when you are pondering God's word? These questions reflect types of spiritual temperaments recognized by Gary Thomas in his book *Sacred Pathways: Discover Your Soul's Pathway to God*.

I can make the most sense out of my spiritual journey as traveling the pathway of loving God with the mind. Thomas calls this the way of the intellectual. I am also an Activist who likes to try things out to see which way the Spirit is leading. But these pathways are very different from what works for most others, especially the Enthusiasts and Caregivers.

Yet unfortunately it is the Intellectuals who have provided most of the leadership in traditional church bodies. Martin Luther was a university professor and John Calvin a highly sophisticated lawyer. Their church bodies have little room for Enthusiasts, Caregivers and Contemplatives. Lutherans in recent decades doubled down on liturgical ritual and symbols. We have actually narrowed our appeal to focus on one small segment of the general population.

For those who want to get closer to God, the usual encouragement is to set aside time for a devotion and prayer in the early morning. That does not work well for me. As near as I can tell, true morning people are only about fifteen percent of the population. I get frustrated with two-paragraph devotions because I want to dig deeper. I have trouble sticking with a rigid discipline. Yet I find that my conversation with God flows freely during the day.

Call to mind the popular image from Revelation 3 of Jesus standing at the door of a house with a lantern in one hand and knocking on the door with the other. He says, "if anyone hears my voice and opens the door, I will come in and eat with him, and he with me." In his popular book *Prayer* Lutheran theologian Ole Hallesby uses this image to describe how Jesus frequently comes to us to start a conversation. He initiates it and if we respond in our thoughts, we have entered prayer.

But strictly speaking it's not Jesus knocking. Jesus Christ ascended to sit at the right hand of the Father. Jesus told his disciples that he won't leave them as orphans. He promised to send the Holy Spirit to teach and remind believers what he had told them. The Spirit is his Spirit. That's Christ's Spirit who enters your thoughts as your day goes along. Next time he knocks spend some time talking with him about whatever else is going on in your mind. That's very valuable prayer time.

What do you think your spiritual temperament? What kind of experiences help you feel especially close to God?

Chapter 5

Waiting on the Spirit

By God's grace, the Spirit changes us. How do we get more of the Spirit's gifts? The answer is to put yourself in the Spirit's work-place—the fellowship of believers gathered around God's word. Some practices are basic. We can do others that stretch our trust and help us learn self-denial.

13. Jesus Explains What the Spirit Can Do in Your Life

19. Practice Denying Yourself

25. Practice Trusting God in a New Venture

31. Practice Giving Witness to Your Spiritual Experiences

37. Practice Conversational Prayer

43. Do You Want a Better Prayer Life?

49. Practice Mindfulness

Jesus Explains What the Spirit Can Do in Your Life

On the evening we call Maundy Thursday, as told by John, Jesus gathered his eleven disciples around a table, perhaps like your dining room table with all the extensions inserted. Judas had left. Jesus had a long, meandering discussion with those who remained about what was going to happen.

Our church has celebrated the Christian Passover several times on Holy Week. Last time it was led by an Israeli member of Jews for Jesus. The Jewish Passover _seder_ format calls for drinking four cups of wine. The third is the cup of redemption, which is when we assume Jesus consecrated the wine and bread to be his blood and body. I noticed last time that after those four cups I was feeling rather mellow. Imagine that as the mood of those twelve gathered around that table.

Jesus told them, "I will ask the Father, and he will give you another Counselor to be with you forever—the Spirit of truth. The world cannot accept him because it neither sees him nor knows him. But you know him, for he lives with you and will be in you. I will not leave you as orphans.

The key term in Greek is _paraclete_, rendered as "counselor" above but better translated as advocate, like a lawyer who stands beside you and presents your case. In his first letter, John uses that word to describe Jesus as our advocate before the Father. So in that one _word paraclete_ we have the job description for Jesus and the Spirit. In the 143 references to the Spirit in Paul's letters, only seventeen us the title "Holy" Spirit. Six refer to Christ's Spirit. So Jesus was teaching about "his" Spirit to come.

*

A few verses later in John 14, Jesus teaches that the Advocate, the Holy Spirit, whom the Father will send in my name, will teach you all things and will remind you of everything I have said to you. The most used symbol for the Spirit is the dove that came down from heaven and sat on Jesus' shoulder at his baptism. I envision the Spirit as sitting on my shoulder whispering godly thoughts into dimension in your worldview, you need also to envision the Enemy sitting on the other shoulder.

Here is how I wait on the Spirit. I go about my day hearing whispers of the Spirit in one ear and the Enemy whispering thoughts into the other. This makes for interesting discussion in my head as the day unfolds. I try to "keep in step with the Spirit", as Paul encourages in his letter to the Galatians on the fruit of the Spirit.

Probably the most helpful part of Jesus' discussion with his followers is his promise, "I will not leave you as orphans." This is a revolutionary truth for classic Protestant theology that basically ignores the Third Person of the Trinity. Calvinists emphasize the First Person, the Father. Lutherans emphasize the Second Person, the Son. The Third Person just does not fit into their understanding of the triune God active today.

Classic preaching expands on our duty as Christians and gives strong encouragement to become more Christ-like. But it usually leaves us on our own to get from where we are to where God would like us to be. It leaves us as orphans.

Jesus' promise to send his Spirit to change us is what I call the additional good news, the forgotten Gospel. It is truly revolutionary for traditional Protestants. Paul tell us about how the fruit the Spirit works, that is, what is the product of the Spirit's work in our individual lives. The Spirit grows within us more, love, joy, patience kindness, goodness, faithfulness, gentleness and self-control. Is there anybody who does not want more of those qualities?

The first Good News is that by grace we have eternal salvation when we accept the Second Person who advocates our case before the First Person. The additional good News is that we are not on our own to become more Christ-like. The First and Second Persons send the Third Person, the Spirit, to change our human spirit, our motivations. This forgotten Gospel is that by grace the Spirit comes to help us grow closer to God and to experience more love, joy, and peace and the other qualities that make our lives more abundant.

We are saved by grace to live by grace—joyfully. Pray that the Spirit comes and makes that happen in you.

Practice Denying Yourself

In the six GROWTH practices I have identified, O is the first stretch practice: **O**pt for Self-Denial (at least once a week). These practices were introduced in Blog 9: **G**o to God in Worship and Prayer, **R**eceive God's Word for You, **O**pt for Self-denial, give **W**itness To Your Spiritual Experiences, **T**rust God in a New Venture, **H**umble yourself before God.

In my personal walk with the Lord, Opting for Self-Denial has been the most productive stretch practice.

Jesus told the rich young man to sell all his possessions and then follow him. He told the disciples that anyone who would follow him must deny him or herself and take up the cross daily. Those weren't commands; they were challenges.

The rich young man wouldn't even consider giving up anything he owned; he went back to his old way of life. It is the willingness to consider this challenge of doing without that is most important. The disciples continually struggled with what they wanted to hang on to from their lives before Jesus called them.

We, too, struggle with how to rise to the counterintuitive challenge of losing your life so you may save it rather than trying to save your life and in the process losing it. It is a riddle that is fully understood only when the Spirit opens our eyes.
*

Understand self-denial to mean not insisting on receiving what is rightfully yours in a relationship but voluntarily giving up something important to you at that moment. Such an act of self-denial, or of losing something from your life, can be a powerful reminder of what you gain as a follower of Christ, thus saving your life by losing it.

Paul did not give commands to his fellow workers and his churches. He pointed out where they should head in specific situations and told them to figure out how to get there. He was not big on rule-making. But he continually emphasized motivations as more important than behaviors. To him it was clear that the Holy

Spirit can and does change human spirits. I interpret human spirits as what we now can call human motivations. He refers to the Spirit 143 times in his letters. The fruit of the Spirit consists of the changed emotions that bring love, joy, peace, patience, kindness, goodness, faithfulness, goodness and self-control into a believer's life.

Paul told the Ephesians to "submit to one another out of reverence for Christ." That is, realize who you are in Christ and act accordingly. Such an intentional act of submission can be especially difficult between husband and wife. When one or the other is argumentative, the natural tendency is to want to defend yourself or your view. That's an opportunity to Opt for Self-Denial by not carrying the discussion on any further. As a conscious act, that can be an exercise in self-denial that has spiritual value.

I am not advocating self-denial and constant submission as a lifestyle. Such might emerge later. But to start, consciously try an act of self-denial or intentional submission once a week. Notice how you feel about it. Deriving benefit from such acts involves being open to the Spirit's influence. See what happens.

I chose O of Opt for self-denial as the key verb for this act of growth in the Spirit. Such an act of self-denial is in your power. Doing it may involve overcoming a basic fear that something bad will happen to you. Face it as a challenge to put your trust in God.

Have you had times when you consciously Opted for Self-Denial?

Practice Trusting God in a New Venture

The fifth of the GROWTH practices I am presenting is to Trust God in a New Venture. Challenge yourself to get out of your comfort zone and do something new and different to help God's Kingdom come in some person's or group's life. This is what you are asking for in the Lord's Prayer. As Luther explains, "The kingdom of God comes indeed without our prayer. But we pray in this petition that it may come in and through us, also."

A basic part of discipleship is to let yourself be drawn Close to God. The Spirit does this when you trust him to bless your new kind of effort, especially when it seems beyond your ability to accomplish. Stretch.

　　*

The classic example is commit yourself to increasing your offering by one or two percent. See what happens. Will you get through the year financially OK? If so, try increasing it the next year until you work yourself up to a 10% tithe. See if you can live that way. Can you feel a higher trust level and Close to God? Pastors notoriously don't like to preach stewardship sermons. Make it a sermon on being drawn Closer to God. That should be the essence of a pastor's ministry.

I am a missions pastor, and I lead many members on mission trips to other countries, especially Haiti. Often are the times I hear someone afterward declaring that mission was a life-changing experience. For the first-timer this means they learned to trust and thus overcome fear. It also usually means they have encountered true poverty for the first time, changing their perspective on their blessings from God.

Marketer's talk about liminality or threshold experiences. This is a new perspective on something that opens up new understandings, like standing on the threshold of a different door for a new perspective on a room. Try some different perspectives on your Christian life and respond to new opportunities you recognize.

Trusting God in a new venture is at the heart of the very popular study *Experiencing God* by Henry Blackaby. It has been translated in 49 languages and sold more than 7 million copies. Blackaby writes especially for Baptists, who in their Calvinist heritage are not used to talking about the Holy Spirit at work today. Where he says God, we can in most cases say God in the Third Person, the Holy Spirit.

Blackaby teaches seven realities: **1.** God is at work around you, **2.** God pursues a continuing love relationship with you that is real and personal, **3.** God invites you to become involved with him in his work, **4.** God speaks by the Holy Spirit through the Bible, prayer, circumstances, and the church to reveal himself, his purposes and his ways, **5.** God's invitation for you to work with him leads you to a crisis of belief that requires faith and action, **6.** You must make major adjustments in your life to join God in what he is doing, **7.** You come to know God by experience as you obey him and he accomplishes his work through you.

His discovery experience came when planting a church. Things didn't go as he anticipated.

For me moving cross country to plant a church brought a new threshold for my perspective on God. It also provided a profound experience of God when my major plans produced no results, and I faced personal failure. I had hit the Wall, as described in Blog 34. I experienced a new kind of deep conversation with God that led to an ongoing interest in studying prayer.

You don't have to move away to challenge your trust in God. Give encouragement to a store clerk who is having a bad day. Organize a service project to help a neighbor in need. Stretch yourself out of you comfort zone in a new way to help God's kingdom here and now. The Spirit will work in you a new level of love, joy and peace.

Can you recall a situation in which you gained a new perspective on your relationship with God?

Practice Giving Witness To Your Spiritual Experiences

The fourth in the GROWTH practices is to give Witness to Your Spiritual Experiences. The six are: **G**o to God in Worship and Prayer, **R**eceive God's Word for You, **O**pt for Self-denial, give **W**itness To Your Spiritual Experiences, **T**rust God in a New Venture, **H**umble yourself before God.

A spiritual experience in your spiritual life could be a fresh insight into your relationship with God, a new conviction of something you feel called to do, a whisper you heard to visit someone at what turns out to be exactly the right time, a time when you felt empowered to reach out to someone, a time of feeling a special level of love, or joy, or peace, or patience. Each of these experiences amounts to a story of what you felt like before, the situation where you had the experience, and then how you felt afterwards.

We can and do talk about the Father in lofty terms of who he is and what he does. We can highlight biblical names that describe his attributes and very generalized verbs that tell what he does, like he is the Creator who provides for us. We can use nouns and generalized verbs to describe who the Son is and what he has done for us, like he is the Redeemer who saves us from our sins.

But the generalized verbs for what the Spirit does contribute little to recognizing him around us now. He calls me by the Gospel, enlightens me with his gifts, sanctifies and keeps me in the faith. The real question is *how* he did this lately. To answer that is to tell a story about what happened to you and how you felt afterwards — preferably in as few words as possible. You are witnessing to how he moved you from a before to an after.

To occasionally throw in the phrase "by the power of the Holy Spirit" too readily becomes a formulaic cliché that flies by without communicating anything.

Giving witness to your experience first of all names it. "This is what the Spirit did to me last year or yesterday." Psychologists point out that to **name** something is to give clear recognition and makes it more memorable. To **share** it makes that experience makes it even more memorable.

If you want to share something for outreach purposes, stories of personal experiences communicate much better than propositional statement, especially when they come in the form Bible passages. Many who are unchurched no longer recognize any special authority of Scriptures and pay little attention. But most people are willing to hear someone else' personal story, especially if it is short. Your personal story of what the Spirit has done in your life is the best evangelistic witness today.

Name and Share are the sub-titles for my book *Your Encounters with the Holy Spirit: Name and Share Them—Seek More* (2014). Something like the GROWTH practices is how to seek more. So are practicing Conversational Prayer (Blog 37), and Practicing Mindfulness (Blog 49).

Have you told anyone about an experience of the Spirit you have had?

Practice Conversational Prayer

She said she enjoyed reading about the saints in college. "Which ones?" I asked. Saint Francis of Assisi came to her mind. Then she added, "and that guy who prayed while he was washing dishes in a monastery." "That would be Brother Lawrence," I noted. She added, "It was new to me that I could pray while doing other things. My life is so busy I just can't get the morning time for devotion and prayer that I know I should take."

In the 17th century, Lawrence was an illiterate brother in a monastery who prayed while he washed dishes. Two monks wrote down his reflections in a book known as *Practicing the Presence of God*. It's now a classic in spiritual literature.

For many Christians, personal prayer is best done at a certain time set aside for that purpose, usually in the morning. Many read prayers written by others. But research I did based on 548 responses from traditional Protestants showed that nine out of ten did most or some of their praying while doing other things, such as jogging, driving, waiting for appointments, or doing routine chores.
*

Call this conversational prayer—talking with God about what is on your mind at that time. Call the alternative formal prayer. Which is better? A case can be made for conversational prayer. Paul challenged the Thessalonians to "be joyful always, *pray continually*; and give thanks in all circumstances." This is the kind of life God wants for his people. Who would not want to live joyfully and thankfully this way?

A character in George Barnano's *The Diary of a Country Priest* recommends plugging away at formal prayer with this explanation, "If you can't pray, at least say your prayers! This is not Christian prayer at its best, but true prayer may arise out of it."

Half of all the respondents in my study reported that in their prayers they regularly experience a deep sense of peace and feel the strong presence of God. Half described their prayers as the most satisfying experience in their lives. I almost overlooked this amazing percentage in all the data. Who would have guessed that half of traditional Christians would describe prayer as the *most* satisfying experience in their life?

In our day, Bradley Hanson notes that "Prayer is more than reciting specific prayers—it is communicating with God, the communion with God that enables us to become more nearly our true selves. So prayer is not a technique that can be mastered. Learning to pray involves learning to trust God in all circumstances. It is always the Lord who teaches us to pray. Of course the Lord uses Scriptures and the lives, words and experiences of others as pointers and guides, but ultimately the real teacher of prayer is God."

Only one out of those many respondents described prayer as a duty, along with the confession that he was not fulfilling it. He was reflecting the Lutheran tradition, expressed by a 20th century theologian who opined in a very Germanic way that "Where there is a willingness to pray it is necessary that the time devoted to that purpose be carefully regulated and the regulations strictly adhered to, or prayer will practically end in omission, as a result of the slothfulness and luke-warmness of our nature."

Even though a prominent theologian, that man didn't have a clue about how the Holy Spirit works today. Like Christ standing and knocking at the door in Revelation 3, Christ's Spirit now frequently knocks on the door of the believer's heart. When we respond in our thoughts, we are launched into the conversation with God called prayer.

Traditional Protestants lost sight of how the Holy Spirit is active around us today. The story of how that happened is long, best told at another time, but the resulting gap in our heritage leaves us much impoverished today. We simply don't believe what Jesus and Paul told us about the one whom we now call the Third Person of the Trinity. We have much to learn from those who take the Spirit more seriously today.

What is your experience with conversational prayer?

The Path To a Better Prayer Life

It took a while for me to realize the significance of the 51 percent among the other percentages in the table. Slightly more than half agreed that "prayer is the most satisfying experience in my life."

The question was deliberately asked in the extreme form—"the most satisfying experience of my life"—to discourage easy affirmation. Yet 51 percent could mark agreement. Sources of satisfaction aren't hard to find in the data. Here are the percentages of those who report they regularly have the following experiences:

- Fifty-five percent experience a deep sense of peace during prayer.
- Forty-five percent feel the strong presence of God.
- Thirty six percent receive what they regard as a definite answer to a specific prayer request.
- Twenty-four percent receive what they believe to be a deeper insight into a spiritual or biblical truth.
- Twenty percent feel divinely inspired or "led by God" to perform some specific action.
  *

A deep sense of *peace* is the most prevalent experience during prayer. Over half the respondents reported that this peace "usually" happens to them. Almost half also usually felt the strong presence of God during prayer.

Receiving answers to prayer is a form of experiencing *power*—the ability to have an impact on people or circumstances around you. About a third "usually" have the reinforcement of seeing clear answers to specific prayer requests.

My book *How the Spirit Shapes Prayer (2017)* is based on research I did among a random sample of ordinary Lutherans from 105 congregations across the country. In it I provide specific descriptions of these outcomes offered by respondents.

For example Janice Benson is a mother of young children and an accounting instructor who sets aside times "to play the piano and sing my prayers to God. I do this in the evening before bed. I think I feel closest to God in prayer."

A woman who chose anonymity commented, "I am often moved to tears during prayer, either with joy or fear. I guess I always feel the love of our Lord while praying, which does make it the most satisfying experience of life!"

An elderly woman commented, "I kept asking God to change my husband (who has multiple health problems) and help him. Only when I prayed that he would change me did my help come and then in abundance. Our daily living is now peaceful and happy (we laugh more, too). I have much greater patience, love and strength. Thanks be to God."

Experiencing the benefits of peace and power amounts to finding that prayer makes a difference—either in oneself or in somebody or something else. As can be observed in the percentages, those who experience such differences are more likely to report greater satisfaction from prayer. Those who more frequently experience satisfaction in prayer are in turn likely to pray more often. The path to a better prayer life goes from experiencing personal benefits to deriving greater satisfaction to doing it more frequently

Simply deciding to pray more frequently in itself probably won't yield a better prayer life. A better place to start is to look directly for those experiences. These come at the initiative of the Spirit. You can receive more of these benefits by placing yourself in the Spirit's workshop—believers gathered around God's Word and sharing their experiences. There the knocking of Christ's Spirit at the door of the heart becomes more evident, especially when you know what you are looking for.

Practice Mindfulness of Biblical Promises

About 3,000 years ago the Psalmist wrote, "Blessed is the man whose delight is in the law of the Lord, and on his law he *meditates* day and night." The writer was referring to being mindful of God's Word.

About 500 years later in China the Buddha (the Awakened One) founded the Buddhist movement, the way of those who are awakened. He emphasized mindfulness as the key to enlightenment.

Christian monks from early on in the world-wide Christian movement practiced mindfulness in their routine chanting the Psalms all the way through many times a month. They focused on Scripture many times a day. Their way of life always struck me as boring to the nth degree. Yet it apparently held personal satisfactions that attracted large numbers of Christians to the monastic movements from the 6th century until recent decades in America.

Psychologist today are re-discovering the value of mindfulness in coping with the challenges of modern living. Their practices have been taken from the Buddhist traditions. Yet the basics apply equally well to meditating on God's Word.

Here is what I have learned from psychologist Ronald Siegel in his lectures and book on *The Mindfulness Solution: Everyday Practices for Everyday Problems.*
    *

Some of Siegel's observations are:

- Mindfulness can be cultivated.
- Mindfulness can help us see and accept things as they are.
- Mindfulness can help us loosen our painful preoccupation with "self."
- Mindfulness frees us to act more wisely and skillfully in every-day decisions.

Ronald Siegel reports research showing that subjects who are distressed tend to have more activity in the right pre-frontal lobes, while subjects who are generally content and have fewer negative moods tend to have more activity in the left pre-frontal lobe. New research shows a relationship between mindfulness meditation and changes to the actual physical structure of the brain. There is support for the conclusion these mindfulness practices dramatically change a persons' mind.

Siegel distinguishes between

concentration practices, which teach how to focus the mind to observe mental phenomena clearly, and

mindfulness practices that use concentration to actively examine how the mind works—in particular to observe how the mind creates unnecessary suffering or making ourselves unhappy by constantly seeking pleasure and trying to avoid pain.

A big part of mindfulness with many practitioners is having a mantra, a sound or phrase to help concentrate the mind. This is a practice that is easily satired, as you have probably seen it done in movies. Among Catholics this practice is called centering or contemplative prayer.

I do think ordinary Christians have favorite mantras to focus their thinking. Many are displayed prominently on wall plaques in the home. From years of visiting homes and hearing Christians' side comments, I think these four are the most common biblical promises that serve as mantras:

- I can do all things through him who *strengthens* me. (Focus on "strengthens")

- In all things God *works for the good* of those who love him.

- For I know the plans I have for you, *plans to prosper* you and not to harm you.

- Those who have hope in the Lord will renew their strength, they will *soar* on wings like eagles.

Martin Seligman, the psychologist who pioneered the study of happiness, observed that "our field has focused on how to move people from 'minus five to zero'. Most of us hope for more. " The Holy Spirit can be at work in biblical mindfulness. He can take believers from Stages 3 to 4 to 5.

Chapter 6

Culturally Shaped Experiences of the Spirit

The social cultures that shape how we communicate and understand ourselves change over time, especially in America now. To be effective, church cultures over the centuries have changed. This involves seeing beyond our current traditions to remain open to the Spirit's movement.

14. Do Your Kids Know That Human Life Is Sacred?

20. Ethnic Churches by the Third Generation

26. Transcendent and Immanent Church Cultures

32. Learnings from the One Non-Ethnic Church in Tremont

38. Suburban Ministries Need To Leave Village Culture Behind

44. Focus on Your Congregations' Culture50. Big 50.

50. Big Changes in American Culture Are Coming

Do Your Kids Know that Human Life Is Sacred?

When I was a Navy Reserve chaplain billeted to a unit in St. Louis, I would be called on to do funerals for Vietnam casualties and also for veterans who requested a Navy funeral. One of those was an old master chief petty officer who gave no indications of spiritual life or admirable qualities. I complained to a Jesuit chaplain friend about how uncomfortable that made me. He set me straight. That man was created in the image of God. His body deserves to be treated with dignity. Do your duty.

That was a fresh insight to me about the meaning of the Genesis statement that God created humans in his image. Scholars debate exactly what that image and likeness consists of. At a minimum it means humans and their God-created bodies are special and different from the rest of creation. The word for that is sacred—set apart to be treated with dignity. The Tomb of the Unknown Soldier in Arlington Cemetery is sacred space for Americans and is given the dignity of a round-the-clock honor guard.

*

Our nation now has two different cultures with strong opinions about the value of human life. Evangelical Christians have advanced the Pro-Life cause against the Pro-Choice movement for legalized abortion. The core issue, of course, is whether a fetus in early pregnancy is human life or just tissue not yet alive. Should an unborn child be given the dignity and protection our law gives to all humans who live and breathe? Of course.

We church people need to recognize that we live in an American society where increasingly citizens no longer believe that there is a real God to whom we are accountable because he created us. As Luther explains in his Small Catechism, God created, preserves and protects me. We need to take that biblical God very seriously. If you approach life with the evolutionary assumption that humans are just the most advanced species of animals, then belief in that biblical God is optional. That has significant consequences for how people live their lives.

On Google I came across this statistic about the percentage of Americans who believe the biblical creation account. Of the World War II generation, 60% believe they were created. Of the baby-boom generation, the figure is 30%. Guess what the percentage is for the millennials, the youngest generation of adults. This study came up with the figure of only 1%. When I relayed this figure in a sermon, there was a loud gasp from someone.

Surely that figure is too small. I suspect whoever did the asking had in mind a specific theory about how God did it. To me *how* he did it is just not important; *that* he did it is crucial. I suspect the percentage of millennials who accept the biblical account may be more like 10-15%. That is still an amazingly low figure.

Do your own survey of young adults and whether they live with biblical assumptions. Where would they ever learn the biblical worldview? The official theory in our schools is that God does not exist and human life is just an extension of animal life. They could get the historic biblical view only from Christians and their churches.

Include in your informal survey of teens a question about how many have ever been in a church, and if so how many had just superficial exposure. You will be amazed. Of course the Bible account is heavily stressed in our confirmation classes. Yet many of our own youth drift away because they really do live with the assumption that God is optional.

Probably the best way for us elders to engage youth in this life-defining discussion is to insist that life is sacred, and then challenge them to define what that means.

How many young adults today do you think live with the conviction that being created in the image of God makes human life sacred?

What is your experience with youth and young adults who consider God to be optional in their lives?

Ethnic Churches by Their Third Generation

I did some research on the 18 churches in the historic, now gentrifying inner-city Cleveland neighborhood of Tremont, where I grew up.

On a Sunday when I looked in on these churches, Iglesia Neuva Vida had about 450 going in and out during their two-hour service. Their new building is located on property that used to be a funeral home. It's on the same block where I grew up in the parsonage of St. Matthew Lutheran. That red brick church building has been occupied for 35 years now by Iglesia de Christo-Sinai. They occupied it after my home church closed its doors in 1976 because of declining attendance and offerings, as the members of that formerly German community moved to the suburbs.

Despite my father's creative and energetic ministry to the new community of former West Virginians and to residents in the public housing projects in Tremont, St. Matthew could not keep its doors open. Both Iglesia Neuva Vida and Iglesia de Christo are on that same block that has become the center of the Puerto Rican community in Cleveland. There are two other Hispanic churches in Tremont as well.

*

Tremont has five Roman Catholic churches. Best attended was St. Michael the Archangel, with 80 in the English service and 300 in the noon Spanish service. I used to walk by this German-rooted church every day on my way to school.

The biggest facility belongs to St. John Cantius, with English and Polish services. St. John Cantius has long held a special place in my memory. In my senior year at Lutheran High School, the Cleveland Press ranked 51 high schools in the Cleveland area. We were 50th. St. John Cantius saved us from being at the very bottom. St. Augustine, midway through the half mile separating St. Michael and St. John, was built by and served Italians. Close by it is a Korean Catholic Church, occupying a building vacated by an earlier Catholic congregation.

Tremont is unique for how many Orthodox churches are there, with their onion dome steeples. St. John Syrian Orthodox's service was standing room only with about 200 in attendance. St. Theodosius Russian Orthodox Cathedral is proud to have become the seat of authority for Russian Orthodox churches in North America. On the far north end of Tremont is Annunciation Greek Orthodox Church. St. Vladimir Orthodox's building is vacant because the congregation moved to a first ring suburb south of Cleveland. The memberships of these Syrian, Russian, Ukranian and Greek churches are still being replenished by immigrants coming from their homelands.

One other kind of ethnic church is also in Tremont. This is the Mega Church, which is predominantly black. It's another church I walked by every day to school, but it was different then. Judging by their website, the people of this church seem to be well-educated and are trying to do ministry in up-to-date ways. Attendance was about 200.

Why call these churches ethnic? Ethnicity is usually based on language, which is very apparent among the churches in Tremont. But more basic is a shared culture. One of the insights offered among the Church Growth principles of Donald McGavran is that people usually like to go to church with people like themselves. When that statement was first offered 40 years ago, it seemed awful to people wanting to promote integration. But it is a fact that won't go away. The only place where truly integrated churches can usually be seen is near a university, where education is the common denominator.

What I see in Tremont is demonstration of the third and fourth-generation cycle of language-based ethnic churches. They can survive and even thrive the first two generations. By the third generation, the children don't know the language anymore and have considerably reduced loyalty to that old culture as they feel more at home in the new broader culture.

The second ring suburbs of Cleveland, where my church Royal Redeemer is located have mostly third-generation adults who are open to any church that serves their needs well. We have several steady participants who won't take up formal Lutheran membership until their Catholic Grandmother dies.

What is the common social denominator of the believers attending your congregation?

Transcendent and Immanent Church Cultures

Transcendent means beyond or above ordinary experience. Immanent means close to ordinary experience.

Mainline churches emphasized a transcendent experience that is very different from normal work life happening in buildings different from ordinary (sanctuaries with stained glass windows) and in special clothing (gowns and Sunday-best) with organ music. Sunday was to be a weekly uplifting experience, fondly remembered by older Christians. In a word, transcendent worship is "formal." It is highly structured.

Younger Christians today look for immanent experiences closely related to their normal daily life. They are comfortable meeting in buildings that have other uses. In our case we meet for contemporary worship in a large gym with basketball hoops that are folded up out of the way for worship. Many congregations meet in sections of a mall. Clothing is casual, including that of the leader. Music is with guitars and drums, much like what they hear in popular music. "Informal" is a very appropriate summary of the style.

*

These two attitudes often conflict in a congregation that has both styles, even when the sanctuary service continues as it was. Some of our older members still call the gym service with a praise band a "hootenanny." These are two different church cultures. Those in the older culture can easily be offended with attempts to start a new culture, with conflict almost inevitable. The old-timers feel no longer appreciated. When Royal Redeemer started the new culture in 1990, we lost an organist, an associate pastor and a handful of members.

I witnessed the beginning of the new that year. It wasn't very good. As I told the pastor, I wouldn't come back for that. It took five years to become a decently moving experience. It took fifteen years, including a change of staff, to get really good. It's like learning a new language, because it is a new and different culture.

Over the years of teaching new member classes, I would ask what attracted them to Royal Redeemer. By far, the word used was the informality of the services. We have settled into the pattern of about two thirds of the attendees in the contemporary service and one third in the traditional.

Managing the transition from one church culture to two takes wise, trustworthy leadership. Senior Pastor Jim Martin had established trust through his previous eight years of loving ministry before starting the change. He was in place for 32 years during growth of staff (from 10 to 90) and fund raising for and planning eight million dollars of capital improvements. He raised the money, and as Administrative Pastor I got to spend it. Those were great years. I am deeply indebted to Jim for finding a role for me.

Our main topic is experiencing the Holy Spirit. Such feeling are associated with "trigger" symbols and relationships. Transcendent worship pulls all sorts of triggers for spiritual experiences. For worshipers raised in traditional churches, the gowns, building symbols, order of service and hymns bring association from their past. If those are good feelings, they come back for more. Often they cannot verbalize why. Many become very protective of the symbols that mean so much to them in their relationship to God.

Transitioning from an old to a new church culture inevitably raises the problem of the second and third generations. The old triggers don't work for them as much anymore. They may have found the old culture boring and have no positive or even have negative associations they are trying to escape. When they feel the need to tend to their relationship with God, they naturally look for and gravitate to the kinds of worship young adults their age from a similar social culture are experiencing.

What is the future for traditional worship? Not good. Face it. That old culture is dying. Those young adults without a traditional background are often attracted to it on rebound from their experiences in Evangelical and Pentecostal churches. Many are in Lutheran seminaries, resisting any change to what they have learned to value. They are not being taught even basic skills for leading and preaching in contemporary worship. What is the future for those seminaries? Not good.

Learnings from the
One Non-Ethnic Church in Tremont

I have commented previously on discoveries from the 18 churches in the gentrifying Tremont neighborhood in center city Cleveland. The one non-ethnic church is Scranton Road Bible Church. As a kid I walked by it on the way to school. It is still in the same building, but they are in the midst of doubling the size of their facility by adding a gym/worship center. Also they have increased their parking by buying and demolishing some of the houses that were there on my daily walk as a school child.

This church's average attendance now is 200–250. When I looked in, the attendees appeared well integrated. I know from conversations in other settings that they are known for their community outreach.

Two large suburban churches are providing much of the funding for their current construction. Therein lie several lessons for doing urban ministry today,
*
Very few center city urban churches today are able to build up a congregation with just the resources of their own members. People with middle and upper incomes have mostly moved out to the suburbs. Those that remain in the inner city have mostly low income. A parallel observation, by the way, is that center-city communities typically have lost their naturally gifted leaders. Those that can lead usually earn higher income and join the movement to housing in the suburbs.

A corollary is that to spread the Gospel in center cities, suburban Christians need to step up to provide leadership and funding. Among the Lutherans I know, it is very hard for first and second generation suburbanites to think of movement back into the city, which they see as dangerous. Their natural orientation is to move further out from the city.

Another corollary is that suburban evangelistic congregations should add to their programming deliberate efforts to build up urban ministries. That usually means adding such ministries to their more comfortable suburban programs. That takes intentional leadership to expand beyond the handful who on their own accept that responsibility.

Beyond these basics, I want to add my story about one of those supporting suburban congregations, Cuyahoga Valley Community Church. It is located in one of the second-ring suburbs targeted for my church plant. I was told it was the fifth attempt to plant a Southern Baptist congregation there. They did better when they dropped Baptist from their identity and became a community church doing contemporary worship.

Cuyahoga Valley had a growing worship community planted in the suburb's high school auditorium three years before I came to plant a Lutheran church. I, by the way, also dropped "Lutheran" from the sign of our plant, thinking we were still too ethnic to attract non-Lutherans. The LCMS logo was on the sign for those who wanted to know. My successor put "Lutheran" back into their public name, reasoning that it projects stability.

I saw CVCC as competition, but I wasn't much of a competitor. I had come straight from academia and didn't know what I was doing. I learned bass guitar so I could be part of the three person praise team and head off the conflict so common with praise teams. We didn't start getting good until a former professional singer took leadership. When we finally got a beat, two families of the original group quit because this kind of "contemporary" was more than they could handle.

Observation: In planting a church, don't even think about starting public worship without a competent praise team. Ideally the sponsoring church should be raising up lots of musicians to use their talents for this mission purpose. Ideally the mother church should send at least 100 of their members to be the core of the new congregation.

What are your thoughts about how best to help a struggling congregation in the center city?

Suburban Ministry Needs to
Leave the Village Culture Behind

When I was a business school professor, I taught the senior capstone course Strategic Management. I still read the *Wall Street Journal* and *Business Week* to stay up with how corporations are changing their strategies for keeping up with the fast-paced changes in technology.

For example, it is amazing how much impact Amazon has had on their competitors and is forcing big changes in other retailers. Many retailing jobs are already gone, and more will disappear as stores close and chains retrench. A similar reorganization is happening in churches under pressure from the community churches.

Strategy comes from the Greek word *strategos*, the general in charge of an army. That general determines when and where to fight the battle and then positions his troops to his best advantage. That's strategy. Tactics are how the various units then achieve their assignments.

*

It has been very frustrating for me over the last 30 years to realize how few pastors and church leaders have any inkling that so many church bodies today are carrying out a strategy developed centuries earlier. Most churches that still value their European heritage are implementing a village strategy. We really need to move on to a suburban strategy for ministry among people who do not know each other and judge congregations by what they experience there.

As anyone knows who has lived in small town, their social culture is very different from the suburbs. In a small town everyone knows everyone. There is strong pressure for conformity. In a village, the head that sticks up is likely to be hammered down into conformity. The pastor is under strong pressure to avoid conflict in the village. A church member getting excited about his or her faith would stand out and make the others uncomfortable. Hence keep your prayers to yourself. In my father's day, a pastor was not even supposed to socialize with members of the congregation, lest he show favoritism.

One vestige of a village church mentality in my church body is that it expects guests visiting the congregation to check with the pastor before participating in communion. In a congregation with attendance of 1,000 with perhaps 700 receiving the Lord's Supper, there's no way all pastors can know all the people who show up at the communion rail. We still keep an official roster of baptisms. Until and even into the 20th century, that was the official record of birth that established citizenship. Members going to another congregation are supposed to ask for a transfer, as if a congregation is a club and can transfer your membership to a different branch of the same organization.

Slow-paced village ministry had its place when people lived in rural areas. Half the congregations in old established church bodies today still are in small towns. The cities had many close-knit ethnic communities where a village strategy still made sense until recent decades.

Suburban churches experience considerable turnover and need to have energetic outreach. Guilt is not a good motivator. Suburbanites expect ministries to be done competently with many program alternatives. To do that involves having lots of worker that have to be motivated. Suburbanites feel little social pressure, and guilt is not nearly as good a motivator as in village churches. They value their personal time highly and don't want it wasted.

Strategies are also expressed in the way life together gets organized and what is emphasized. All that together can be described as a congregation's culture. Changing strategies amounts to fine-tuning the existing culture.

A big topic in business schools today is changing corporate culture. Businesses are under immense pressure to figure out how to produce a better product with less cost. Most of this is driven by changes in technology that never seem to end. In my book *Your Encounters with the Holy Spirit* (2014) I present a chapter on basic business school principles for how to implement organizational culture changes.

Amazon is putting immense pressure on traditional retailers. It is the large growing community churches that are putting the competitive pressure on traditional congregations. Many will be faithful to their traditional culture and most likely will die. Those that retain a strong sense of mission will need to focus much more on their unique source of energy—the Holy Spirit.

Focus on Your Congregation's Culture

The dictionary definition of a culture is an integrated pattern of *knowledge*, *beliefs* and *behaviors* that determines what is learned and transmitted to future generations. Most congregations can tell you what they know and believe. But few are aware of how their behaviors form a distinctive church culture. Often, a younger generation sees behaviors that are or are not being done. They are either impressed by what they see and stay. Or they are bored or turned off and leave.

Christian Schwarz is a contemporary German theologian and church researcher. He offers a framework for recognizing and describing a congregation's culture. This is presented in *Natural Church Development: A Guide to Eight Essential Qualities of a Healthy Congregation*. I was impressed by the thoroughness of his theory and understanding of churches in his previous book *The Third Reformation*.

Schwarz and his organization Church Smart offer a Natural Church Development Survey. It consists of ninety-one statements that assess how often a participant does or observes specific behaviors. Up to thirty members of the congregation are asked to fill this out. The result is an assessment of that congregation's church culture that describe eight qualities or characteristics.

He makes no pretense of being objective about what these qualities should look like in a healthy congregation. They are:

empowering leadership	gift-oriented ministry
passionate spirituality	inspiring worship service
functional structures	holistic small groups
need-oriented evangelism	loving relationships

Based on the questionnaires submitted by the congregation members, the church is given a score on each of the qualities, which is compared to the average for the hundreds of other congregations that were studied around the world. Those churches that are way below the average for most of the qualities typically do not survive long. Those that are very high on each typically are exciting churches that are also growing numerically.

You can do your own assessment of your congregation's culture by answering questions like these:

- When a visitor observes a Sunday service, what mood would he or she pick up?
- When someone inquires, "Tell me about your church" what stories are told?
- Who shares leadership of the church with the pastor?
- Who gets recognized and affirmed and for what achievements?
- Does the church have a clear direction for the future, and how well is it known?
- What is the level of creativity and enthusiasm among the participants?
- What does the condition of the physical facility tell about the values of the members and leaders?
- How are decisions made, and how often are they deferred or delayed?
- Do the church people talk mostly about the past or the future?

How to change a corporate culture is a major topic in business schools. Here are some principles that are applicable to churches:

- Changing an organization's culture is anxiety-provoking.
- Strong leadership is needed to change such a culture.
- Culture change inevitably brings conflict between those liking the old and those espousing the new.
- Leaders have to earn the right to be followed in new behaviors.
- Culture trumps vision. Vision is about ideas. Culture is behavior.

What improvements in the behavior of you congregation would you like to see?

Big Changes in American Culture Are Coming

One of the popular books in my seminary days was *The Secular City,* in which Harvey Cox of Harvard Divinity School tried to work out a theology for the "post-religious" age that many sociologists had confidently assured us was coming. Since then, he says some religions seem to have gained a new lease on life. Today it is secularity, not spirituality, that may be headed for extinction. He eats this crow in his *Fire From Heaven: The Rise of Pentecostalism and the Reshaping of Religion in the Twenty-First Century.*

Philip Jenkins offers a big picture view of the future of Christianity worldwide as well as in America. He is Professor of History and Religious Studies at Pennsylvania State University. His book considered here is *The Next Christendom: The Coming of Global Christianity*. He works mostly with demographic projections.

In his many-year demographic overview, he finds that in 1900 Europe, North America and former lands of the Soviet Union accounted for 32% of the world's population. In 2050 that percentage will be down to 10-12%. In the next 50 years, "We will see a spectacular upsurge in Southern populations and a decisive shift of populations to the Southern continents."

"As the nation [America] grows, its ethnic character will also become less European and less White, with all that implies for religious and cultural patterns."
*

 "American society is readily moving from a Black and White affair to a multicolored reality." "In the late 1990s California became the nation's first 'majority-minority' state, in which non-Latino Whites ceased forming an absolute majority of the population."

In Texas, "While the proportion of foreign-born was less than 3 percent in 1960, today it is 25 percent. In the 19th century, Anglos overwhelmed the whole continent, leaving the older Hispanic culture as shrinking islands of language and faith within the U.S. border. In retrospect, those islands now look more like bridgeheads from which new advances would someday occur."

"The Christian presence is powerfully evident in any Asian community in North America. Vancouver has a sizable Asian presence. The greater Vancouver area has around fifty Christian congregations labeled with some Asian ethnic title, such as 'Chinese Pentecostal' or 'Korean Baptist'. That figure does not count distinct services in ethnic languages offered by mainstream Catholic or Protestant churches. In addition, thousands of Vancouver residents of Asian descent attend mainstream Christian services in the English language. A similar picture can be found in Chinatowns and Little Saigons across the United States."

As I was pulling these quotes out of Philip Jenkins' book, I thought of my observations from the Tremont research I did. Of eighteen churches in that historic neighborhood, seventeen had ethnic roots. For almost its entire history, Christianity grew among believers who shared language and cultural identities of many different ethnicities. In America in the 21st century, most of those diverse ethnic roots are disappearing.

Ministering today among people who have no post-ethnic shared identity is a new challenge. Typically now the shared identity is shaped by common problems and yearnings of shared suburban life.

For traditional churches, clearly it is time to shift from a long-gone village mentality to a strategy appropriate to suburban realities. I discussed these two contrasting strategies in Blog 38.

Chapter 7

Organizing the Spirit's Fellowships

Jesus taught that the Spirit is not predictable. Yet life together in fellowships of the Spirit does need structure. The challenge is to adapt institutional structures that remain open to the fresh movement of the Spirit. Many churches made poor organizational decisions in the 20th century that lost focus on the Spirit's energy. We need to get back to the basics of Spiritual energy.

Blogs

15. Your Congregation Is the Top Soil for the Spirit's Work

21. Do You Want Your Church Leaders To Be Shepherds or Builders?

27. The Misunderstanding of the Church

33. Planting Churches the New Way

39. Emerging Alternatives to Seminaries

45. Why Do Some Churches Grow and Others Decline?

51. A Strategy for Supporting Urban Ministries

See Your Congregation as the Top Soil for the Spirit's Work

In his very first parable, the Sower and the Seed, Jesus described the poor soils that were hard, rocky and weedy, and the good soil which produced a bumper crop. Paul thought of the Corinthians as a field where he planted, Apollos watered and God gave the growth. Consider the application of these metaphors in church leadership today.

Eugene Peterson is best known for his paraphrase of the Bible called *The Message*. A pastor's pastor, he describes a congregation as the topsoil for pastoral work. "It is the material substance in which all the Spirit's work takes place—these people, assembled in worship, dispersed in blessing."

"They are so ordinary, so unobtrusively there, it is easy to take them for granted, to quit seeing the interactive energies, and to become so preoccupied in building my theological roads, mission constructs, and parking lot curricula that I start treating this precious congregational topsoil as something dead and inert to be arranged to suit my vision."

"Why do pastors so often treat congregations with the impatience and violence of developers building a shopping mall instead of the patient devotion of a farmer cultivating a field?"

The Apostle Paul described what such ministry of cultivating a field would look like, as he explained in passages that were never fully appreciated by churches and their leaders over seventeen centuries of institutional Christianity.

*

As Paul wrote to the Corinthians, he wanted the believers in his churches to not be ignorant of spiritual gifts. One manifestation of the Spirit is in the variety of talents, special callings and energies that are to be put to work for the common good of the congregation. The second, greater manifestation is the way the Spirit produces faith, hope, love and other such qualities in the lives of believers.

Believe me, the practicalities of administering such gifts are very challenging. The hardest part is finding enough jobs for everybody in their shared congregational life. Ironically, traditional church leaders complain they can't get enough people to fill the all the jobs in their church's committee structure. That is because so many churches today have the wrong theology of church and an outdated understanding of church leadership.

A traditional congregation usually divides itself between clergylike people who do the ministry and everybody else, the laity who support those few with their prayers and offerings. In Paul's understanding, every member is a minister. The job of leaders, including pastors, is to guide and support them in what they are all doing for the common good.

To appreciate Paul's thinking, follow him as in 1 Corinthians 3:10 he from seeing a congregation in organic terms to envisioning it as a building. He regarded himself as the master builder, or literally, the architect for putting all the human pieces together as a temple in which the Spirit brings energy for dynamic ministry.

Most traditional congregations are organized poorly. They have committees trying to determine what others are supposed to do. This is a sure formula for a static church life. In American culture today, each congregation does need a small governance structure to oversee facilities and finances, like a corporate board of trustees. Greater efficiency and effectiveness comes from having a separate ministry structure that takes responsibility to administrate the people doing the basic ministries.

I have learned the following cardinal leadership principle in suburban churches: Don't waste the personal time of those wanting do to a ministry. Get them to work as quickly and directly as possible and give them the necessary support to do well. As congregations get larger, they need to recognize staff ministry developers. Usually these are paid. We have several who don't need to be compensated. We tell staff they should work 40 hours a week plus as many hours as their best volunteers put in.

Has your personal time been used well in your congregation?

Do You Want Your Church Leaders To Be Shepherds or Builders?

The title of Pastor has been popular among Protestants since the mid-18th century. For centuries before then the title was Father, as it still is among Roman Catholics. The Pietists, who were at their peak in the 18th century in Germany and Scandinavian countries, used pastor to reduce the distance between the clergy and the laity, as the social status of clergy grew ever loftier. "Pastor" in Latin means shepherd.

I am surprised that the pastor title is used so extensively even in American Evangelical circles. There are two alternatives. One is "Reverend" and the other is "Preacher." Reverend is used frequently among mainline churches, as Rev. John Doe. I think Pastor is the loftier title, used only for those pastoring a congregation. Rev. applies to all ordained, whether or not they are pastoring.

I am proposing a new title for the leader of a suburban church. Pastor is very appropriate for a village church (see Blog 38)). Jesus self-identified as a shepherd. Paul, however, self-identified as a master builder, and the Greek is *architecton* (1 Corinthians 3:10). A good title for doing ministry Paul's way would be Mb. (Master Builder) or Arch. (Architect). That kind of title is most appropriate for a new suburban strategy.

*

In the Gospels, Jesus used the shepherd analogy eight times, five in his teaching on the Good Shepherd. He used "church" only once. Paul, on the other hand, in his letters implied the shepherd image only once. He used the word for building up fellowship twenty-five times and the word for church 103 times. Jesus discipled his twelve followers and taught the basics of relationships with God and each other. Paul, on the other hand, planted and led local congregations in many cities. He is really the founder of the world-wide Christian church on earth. I enjoy studying how he did that.

Key, I think, is that he thought in terms of a fellowship builder. The Greek word is *oiko-domeo,* to build a house. The *oikos is* literally the physical house, and then by extension the people living in it. The Greeks had no name for family other than *oikos*. By extension, *oikos* became the fellowship we call church, which met for centuries in private homes—house churches. His letters went to the house churches (the fellowships) then existing in large cities.

Most of the twenty-five times Paul used the *oikodomeo* term were in verb form. He was continually encouraging the house churches to "build up the fellowship." I like to put the "up" in the English—to build *up* the fellowship. To the Ephesians Paul writes, "From Christ the whole body, joined and held together by every supporting ligament, grows and builds itself up in love, as each part does its work."

In the same Ephesians chapter, he encourages leaders "to prepare God's people for works of service, so that the body of Christ may be built up." A popular translation is "to equip." In five other New Testament passages where that Greek word is used, the meaning suggests getting something in alignment, organizing. My personal preference is to translate that the purpose of church leaders is "to get God's people organized for works of service."

Centuries of pastors looked at the Latin version "to edify" (*aedos -facare,* with *aedos* as an edifice, a building, with *facio* meaning to make) and translated edification to their advantage, to give spiritually uplifting messages. That rather bland function takes on a whole new meaning when leaders are encouraged to get their people organized for works of service, something that is crucial to a suburban strategy for planting and building churches.

To the Corinthians Paul pointed out that "everything is permissible, but not everything builds up." Accept this maxim: **If what you are about to say and do does not build up the fellowship, don't do it.** Think of how many existing churches would become more attractive if their members took Paul's precept seriously.

What is your reaction to church leadership as building rather than shepherding?

The Misunderstanding of the Church

The understanding of truth and church are fundamental to ministry. A German Protestant professor in Zurich, Emil Brunner, opened up for me new perspectives on each. He is regarded as one of the top four or five systematic theologians of the mid-20th century.

He saw *Truth as Encounter*, the name of his book. In my philosophy days, the theology/philosophy of 13th century Thomas Aquinas seemed the best. At that time it was taught at all Catholic universities. But I didn't find it very productive to adopt categories that Protestants don't understand.

Brunner highlighted that truth is relationships experienced, not doctrine tightly defined. Encountering Jesus is the truth, the way, the life. Life-changing encounters happens in the heart, not just the head. Heart-work is done by the Holy Spirit. As Jesus said, the Spirit will take from what is mine and make it known to you.

The other fundamental new perspective came through his book The *Misunderstanding of the Church*. In his time when most church leaders thought of church, they had in mind church institutions which in Europe were well developed over centuries. They saw the Christian church of the first several centuries as the "primitive" church. The "early" church is a better name. I regard it as the best source for re-learning how to do church more effectively in our times.

*

Emil Brunner was at his peak in the 1950s, when the ecumenical movement was at its height. This was a time when institutional church leaders tried to work out their differences and be united. A few mergers happened, like the one that produced the United Church of Christ. But the movement soon died.

Brunner was telling them they had the wrong understanding of church. It is fundamentally the fellowships brought together by the Holy Spirit. These exist prior to whatever institutional form they take on. He called for a greater appreciation of the freedom the Spirit brings. Some institutional churches seem intent to limit that freedom. Many believers who have learned the Spirit's freedom refuse to have anything to do with institutional churches that are intent on unnecessarily restricting them.

Extending his starting point brings two fresh approaches to organizing the fellowships of the Spirit at the congregational and denominational levels.

There is no biblically prescribed organizational form a congregation should follow. Paul distinguished supervisors and helpers. The Greek words from which we get bishop and deacon were everyday language for those functions. The category of elders was adopted from the synagogues and basically meant recognized, trusted leaders. The category of "clergy" does not exist in Scriptures, nor is there persuasive evidence for a special ordination to that elevated office.

Informal fellowships need some structure to survive. The function of that formalized organization is to look after the health and safety of the underlying fellowship—provide for the spiritual welfare and growth of the participants, resolve conflict, take responsibility for property and plan for the future.

Judging by the declining health of so many traditional congregations, their leaders have not been doing a good job. Most are responsible and mature men and women who are trying to make sensible decisions within the traditional options they recognize. Those who are really failing are the spiritual leaders of churches that have drifted away from recognizing the authority of Scriptures, from which they can draw true spiritual energy rather than rely only on the human energy available to social clubs.

Denominational structures need to leave behind any notion that they are the church. The defining fellowships are at the congregational level. Headquarters exist to help the congregations lead their underlying fellowships. It is foolish to think that a small group of denominational leaders speak for all the million or more believers in their congregations.

In the community church movement the emerging effective congregations don't form highly defined denominations. They develop informal networks with other leaders and congregations who share interests. They may be involved in two or three networks at the same time. This is especially true in mission work.

Planting Churches the New Way

In 1990 I was called to be a mission developer on the staff of the Ohio District of the Lutheran Church—Missouri Synod. I was paid district scale, which with my 23 years since ordination and my educational level was generous. The days of that kind expense for church planting are gone.

Through a providential set of events while teaching my D.Min course on Church Management, at 3:00 pm on Monday, January 15, 1990, I felt convicted that God was calling me to plant a new church in the southern suburbs of Cleveland. That call is very comforting when you go through all the ups and downs of church planting.

Since that start in 1990, I know of only one other successful district church plant. This is out of probably 12 attempts. Nobody has ever counted because, I suspect, they don't want to see the number. From Royal Redeemer, where my work is based, we have had three successful church plants out of four attempts.

Here is what we have learned from our three Royal Redeemer efforts out of four attempts.

*

My definition of success is surviving five years and being financially self-sufficient. I have heard lots of young leaders brag about all the churches they planted. By far, most turn out to be small group Bible studies that soon disappear. Here is what we have learned from our three Royal Redeemer efforts out of four attempts.

Actually, Royal Redeemer was most responsible for the plant I did, which became Community of Hope Lutheran. It was ostensibly sponsored by a local group of congregations. I think all the other nine churches didn't say no, and that was taken for a yes. We had only two of our core group come from those sponsoring churches. Those congregations did give us the names of their members living in the target suburbs. That was the old style of church planting. I don't recall getting any of those to become members of COH. Those that were still going to church were happy where they were.

I preached and pastored there for six years, the last three half-time while I was at Royal Redeemer half-time. I don't think church planting is a full-time job for an energetic ordained pastor.

My successor, Doug Seletzky, was a young man newly recruited by Royal Redeemer for leading the contemporary service. He and I basically traded positions when I went there as Administrative Pastor.

Doug was able to dip into the Lutheran High School alumni network to get attendance up to about 100. That seems to be the minimum to take on real growth dynamics. Twenty years later, with average attendance at about 200, they dedicated their new building in the center of Broadview Heights. One of the reasons they survived so long is that they occupied a deserted dormitory that the church remodeled. Six months after occupying the new building, attendance had gone up to 250.

The second successful plant (surviving at least five years and financially self-sufficient) started about 12 years ago and had two previous planters before the present one. They are now in a rented strip mall remodeled by a previous community church plant that did well. The last time I looked, they had attendance of about 60, including six with motorcycle leathers on. Before his ministry days, the planter of this church had been president of the Christian Motorcycle Association in Cleveland.

The third successful plant is back toward the city. They just celebrated the fourth anniversary of their start. I had gotten to know Dave Walters, their planter, as I led a group from Community of Hope on a Haiti mission. Brought up at Royal Redeemer, he had a life-changing experience in another Lutheran church near Dayton. As he discovered the impact of God's grace, he wondered why no one had ever told him this before. I recognized in him a young man with a passion for outreach. We purchased a former Denny's restaurant that they refurbished into a meeting room that seats 100.

Here are three lessons about church planting. 1. Don't decide to plant and then find a planter. Find the passionate planter first. 2. For all the correct theological reasons, a church is not a building but people. Nevertheless, people in the neighborhood won't recognize a new church until they see a physical presence. 3. Help the plant get that presence. Royal Redeemer did so by buying our church plant ministry a shuttered up former Denny's restaurant that they remodeled

Have you observed a successful church plant in your area? How did they do it?

Emerging Alternatives to Seminary

Traditional state churches inherited a pattern for raising up and ordaining pastors that goes back to medieval churches. Preparation for ministry was done at universities emerging at the major cathedrals. Today the established pattern is an advanced degree from a seminary accessible by only those who have earned a college degree.

Non-traditional churches and their pastors are now raising serious questions about whether this is the best preparation for effective congregational ministry. The issue is whether education first and then ministry is really better preparation than showing effectiveness in ministry and then bringing alongside educational experiences to strengthen that ministry.

Seminary enrollments across the country are in steep decline. One of the explanations is that potential seminarians are getting their training brought to them while doing congregational ministry. Another reason is lack of compelling evidence that academic success leads to effective ministry.

I read a biography of a very successful Evangelical preacher who, starting at age 20, did revival preaching on weeknights as well as Sundays. I reflected on how at that age I was in my dormitory room and classrooms studying Greek, Latin, Hebrew and German. I didn't do any serious preaching until after eight years of post-high school study and also after learning a specialized vocabulary. Who do you think would be the better preacher at holding an audience's attention and speaking the kind of language they understand?

Let me show what the new kind of training looks like.
*

I know of a congregation that raised up three preachers in unconventional ways. Let's call them Al, Bob and Carl. Carl was on the church staff leading a worship team. He knew how to develop leaders. He approached Al about singing on the team. Even though Al did not think he had a good voice, he joined the group. Then Carl encouraged him to play guitar. Al only knew how to play the accordion but did take up guitar. And then Carl left to take a new ministry assignment. Al became the worship leader. First he went for six Sundays to a large community church to study the techniques of their worship team. Al has been leading his church's team now for twenty years.

Al is a communicator. With a radio voice, he had his own daily show on a local Christian radio station. He did stand-up comedy. It made sense to have him preach once in a while in the Saturday evening contemporary service. As more services were added, it made sense for him to preach more often. He has been in the preacher rotation for that church now for about ten years.

Al learned theology and ministry skills by sitting in on prep sessions for the courses Carl was taking in a seminary distance learning program on the way to being ordained. The sessions were led by a seminary-educated former pastor. Bob also sat in. Previously a printer, he had joined that staff ten years earlier as sports minister and confirmation class teacher. At that time the church body had the category of a licensed deacon, who could do all ministries other than consecrating the sacrament. After ten years as a licensed deacon, he qualified for an interview and was approved for ordination. He is a good preacher with a commanding voice who has been in the preaching rotation for ten years.

My overall theme in these Blogs is that American society is swiftly changing in a direction no longer favorable to traditional mainline church bodies and their institutions. They (we) will have to change their church cultures if they want to regain their vigor.

Would your church bring on a proven leader as pastor with the understanding that training will be brought to him?

Why Do Some Churches Grow While Others Decline?

Big changes are happening on the American religious scene. This is my constant theme. Many in the declining traditional Protestant churches often seem perplexed. Why are those community churches growing while we are going down? There is no simple answer, but some explanations are emerging.

In the 1980s and 90s there was a ministry discipline called Church Growth. It grew out of the observations of Donald McGavran, who studied mission movements. His work was popularized by C. Peter Wagner. Both worked out of Fuller Theological Seminary, where I was in the 80s. One of McGavran's key insights was that people don't become believers individually; they do so in groups. Out of this came the controversial homogenous principle. People like to go to church with others like themselves.

In the early 20th century most churches in America were made up of immigrants who shared the same language and home culture. Most remained vibrant through their second generation. By mid-century they were into their third and four generations   Most of these younger members had lost their ethnic loyalty by then. Many did carry on their church loyalty into the suburbs through the 1950s-70s   Their children are the millennials who are no longer in our churches. In retrospect, the churches were coasting on family loyalties. Those days are now gone. To survive, those former ethnic churches need to develop new approaches to ministry.

*

Church Growth advocate C. Peter Wagner wrote like a journalist about the big successful congregations of the day. Implied was that if yours does like they do, you, too, will grow. The market for church growth advice and materials is huge.

The issue fundamentally is whether specific methods and leadership are the real explanation for growth. The best answer would come by researching many, perhaps 100, congregations that claim they are using the featured methods and see what they look like ten years later. Some will have grown very large, most will have stayed about the same, and many will have declined or even collapsed. Indeed many of the church growth "winners" did collapse in following years for a variety of reasons.

Many are the business CEOs who claim personal credit for enviable corporate results. In reality that company may well have hit a unique set of circumstances in the relevant market. Had they come to market a few years earlier or later and had some unique opportunities not appeared, the results would be quite different. Much of the explanation is a few lucky breaks they had. And took advantage of.

I know first-hand the story of the growth and plateau of Royal Redeemer Lutheran in church in North Royalton, Ohio. The then-senior pastor did consciously decide, for authentic mission purposes, that this congregation should reach out more effectively. Because he was highly trusted as a pastor, he could make some basic organization changes. He started a contemporary service in 1990 and lost an organist and assistant pastor in reaction. By the late 90s we were growing at five to ten percent a year.

Usually untold is that a new religious editor for the Cleveland Plain Dealer chose Royal Redeemer for his story about contemporary worship. That story was on the Sunday issue front page with a large photograph of our worship service. Attendance went up by 200 six months later. Also, we received a totally unexpected gift of $1 million dollars that enabled us to build a gym/worshiper center much larger than otherwise.

At about 1,000 in attendance, we stopped growing. One explanation is that the other three large Protestants congregations in our area each opened a new sanctuary in that decade. New sanctuaries almost always result in higher attendance. Old sanctuaries become a competitive disadvantage.

My conclusion? Significant church growth is a special providential blessing of God. When that happens leaders need to run like mad to accommodate future growth.

The Lord giveth and the Lord taketh away. Blessed by the Lord. Meanwhile be good stewards of his special blessings.

The Fellowship Builder's Toolbox

The basic tools for pastoral ministry are Word, sacraments, worship and prayer. In Blog 21 I highlighted the contrast between the traditional shepherd understanding of pastoral ministry and the fellowship building role that the Apostle Paul pioneered and I am advocating. Shepherds and builders approach ministry with different emphases.

For the shepherd pastor, getting the Word proclaimed is sufficient, usually with a 10-15 minute sermon delivered from the pulpit and based on scriptural selections in the pericopies for that year. In contrast, a builder wants to be sure the Word is communicated and understood as well as possible. This means using Power Point slides along with the verbal presentation, delivered as close to the listeners as possible. Builders build sermon series on topics that address listeners' concerns. Start with questions a hearer has in his or her own frame of reference and speak God's truth to that, instead of starting with a scriptural text and getting around to application.

*

How to plan and lead worship has been very controversial in recent decades, although the "worship wars" of the 1990s are basically over. The sides have been chosen. Shepherd pastors emphasize the formal liturgical format for the Divine Service, advocating the Lord's Supper in each service. Builders, on the other hand, gravitate toward the more informal contemporary format, with moments of spontaneity. They often group songs together at the beginning of the worship time and before focusing on the Word. Engaging worship stands in contrast to liturgical worship.

Many shepherd pastors today consider anything with the appearance of "contemporary" to be participation in false doctrine. To their frustration, the other side, which makes use of contemporary forms, goes about its business ignoring the discourse altogether. They have gone on to discussion of ministry topics other than worship.

The two approaches to ministry have different understandings about prayer in church life. Traditional shepherds expect that the pastor does the praying in formal well-constructed prayers at the altar, with the understanding that individuals do their personal prayers at home. Builders see prayer as an opportunity to build fellowship, typically in a time of sharing in small group gatherings. They will often have a formal organized prayer ministry with a prayer chain, an intercessory prayer group, prayer with individuals after the service, or a scheduled service of prayer for healing.

"Spiritual disciplines" are receiving more attention among Protestants, pioneered by Richard Foster in his 1978 book *Celebration of Discipline: The Path to Spiritual Growth*. Dallas Willard probes in greater depth in *The Spirit of the Disciplines: Understanding How God Changes Lives.*

In traditional Lutheran and Episcopalian congregations the primary disciplines are corporate, revolving around worship times and supplemented with events for the whole fellowship. Fellowship builders try to include other disciplines and organized activities, especially small group Bible study and prayer, with many groups meeting in the evening of weekdays. Traditional churches often fill those evenings with committees discussing how *to plan* ministry and meet organizational needs. Builders see those evenings a time *to do* ministry.

Organized mission trips are a good way to build fellowship and deepen understandings of faith active in life. Most of the people I know well at Royal Redeemer participated in missions trips.

One form of ministry that has done well at our church is twice-annual Servant Saturdays, in the spring and fall. We have about 300 individuals, including families, who show up on a Saturday morning for breakfast and three hours of helping elderly in the community, usually with clean-up projects. Most programs slump after few years. This one has maintained its attraction. When you are cleaning up someone else's yard, you face the question of why and affirm your belief that service is basic to the Christian life.

You can read more about these contrasts in my book *Builder Ministry for the 21st Century* (2010).